DATE DUE

Demco, Inc. 38-293

The Jealous Child

Books by Edward Podolsky

MEDICINE MARCHES ON

MUSIC FOR YOUR HEALTH

STOP WORRYING AND GET WELL

YOU AND YOUR TROUBLES

DOCTORS, DRUGS AND STEEL

THE THINKING MACHINE

Editor:

WAR MEDICINE

ENCYCLOPEDIA OF ABERRATIONS

MUSIC THERAPY

The Jealous Child

By EDWARD PODOLSKY, M.D.

*Department of Psychiatry, Kings County Hospital,
Brooklyn, New York*

PHILOSOPHICAL LIBRARY
New York

PRINTED IN THE UNITED STATES OF AMERICA
BY THE HADDON CRAFTSMEN, INC., SCRANTON, PA.

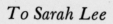

To Sarah Lee

Foreword

Life for all of us is an experience. This experience is quite simple at the beginning, but as life goes on this experience becomes more and more complex. Each of us needs to meet problems and solve them. In working out life's problems we require opportunity for satisfying achievements in an atmosphere of love and understanding.

Living has form and substance, and effective living is not an aimless process, it is an art. Life is not as William James has called it, "a big, blooming, buzzing confusion." Nor is it as some one else has said, "a drowsy reverie, interrupted by nervous thrills." Life is, or should be, ordered, spontaneous, disciplined and free.

Life is not a lonely adventure. Man as an effective human being cannot live by himself alone and for himself alone. He must live in close relatedness with his fellow human beings, his surroundings and with himself. Being in the world is always existence with others. Existence without relatedness to some one or some thing is not possible for a human being possessed of his faculties.

Existence, or being in the world, or in other words, living in relatedness with others, as we must, often results in anxiety, inner tensions, conflicts and emotional stresses. No human being can live out a life time without experiencing some degree of tension, apprehensiveness and other psychic disruptions.

From the first year of life until the last we encounter situations laden with one anxiety or another. Each period in life brings its own particular problems and tensions, and we must be prepared to meet and solve these problems as they present themselves in order to resolve these anxieties and live a happy, tension-free life. Childhood is a period of life filled with many problems that result in stressful situations which bring about uncomfortable emotional reactions.

A child is a body-mind organism. What affects his body affects his mind, and what affects his mind affects his body. Various bodily ills, chronic ailments, malformations, etc., react upon his total personality in such a way as to cause rather intense emotional reactions. A child who is chronically ill, who has some defect which makes him too conspicuous, whose ailment forces him to lead a regimented and restricted life, in time, becomes emotionally disturbed. He feels that he is not like other children; he knows that he lacks something that other children have, and he experiences jealousy in its most virulent form.

Jealousy is an emotional expression that does not exist in a vacuum. It has definite effects on the body-mind system; it tends to disrupt inner harmony, and in some instances cause organ protests, such as upset stomach, dizzy spells and headaches.

The tools for effective living in the child as well as in the adult are rooted in the personality. The effective management of those conditions that result in jealousy and other disrupting emotions calls for mature behavior. Mature behavior and attitudes are an efficient method of maintaining a wholesome, well-integrated personality. Mature behavior is also characterized by flexible adaptation to any given situation. By attaining importance of one kind or another a child attains prestige, ego satisfaction and acceptance. The feeling of rejection is always laden with anxiety, envy and jealousy, and a child by attaining significance also achieves a feeling of usefulness and of being wanted and of belonging. A child who feels that he does not belong is also a jealous child.

In this book I have considered the various conditions which

result in jealousy in a child. These are physical, emotional, social and economic; and under each category I have taken into account specific elements, such as chronic ailments, physical deformities, sibling rivalry, adoption, school segregation, etc. How these conditions result in jealousy are fully considered as well as what can be done to resolve the feeling of jealousy. The jealous child is not a rare phenomenon in our culture. He requires help and guidance. In this book I have endeavored to point out what the parents, teachers and other adults can do for the jealous child.

EDWARD PODOLSKY, M.D.

CONTENTS

CONTENTS

CHAPTER ONE

What Growing Up
Means to a Child

The infant's first experience is a traumatic one; being born is a cataclysmic separation from a world of absolute dependence, quiet comfort and nerveless ease. For nine months the infant lived, grew and developed in a peaceful, satisfying and ideal environment. This was the quiet warmth and comfort of the mother's womb. Without effort or struggle all its wants were gratified. It was the central star in its own private universe. There were no disturbing or alarming changes, no abrupt breaks and no sudden demands to bring about tensions and anxieties. Prenatal life is life at its ideal best. It is the tension-free organismic home to which all human beings yearn to return in times of sharp conflicts.

The first painful contact with the harsh reality of postnatal life is the doctor's slap on the back to stimulate the newly-born child to do its own breathing. He must now put forth some exertion to live; he must make his first attempts to master his new environment. He has lost his omnipotence and his own private universe. He is now one individual in a living, struggling world of two billion others.

Life, from the very beginning, is neatly sectioned into various stages that succeed each other as the years go by. From the very first year of life until old age we have different needs, different points of view, different requirements, different modes of living, different ideas and ideals and different stresses and sources of conflict. Life, from the very beginning, is an ever-changing stream, constantly winding into new territories, unveiling new vistas, new horizons, bringing new experiences, affording physical, mental and emotional growth.

All infants have identical requirements. The first is the need for physical safety which includes protection from hunger, cold, wetness and other disagreeable physical impacts. The second is the need for affection, for being wanted and cared for, of belonging to some one. The third is the need to grow and develop according to his own inherent patterns and rhythms.

All these are essential needs which must be fulfilled in order for the infant to attain his best growth physically, mentally and emotionally. The judicious yielding to the biological needs of the infant will result in the development of a normal healthy child.

Growing up is a difficult process. Even babies must learn to conform to the world about them, and many infants will find this an intolerable process. Under certain conditions it is necessary to modify the demands of the environment upon the infant to ease his daily routines. This, of course, must be done within reason.

Infants grow and develop in a normal and orderly way. At each new stage of development the infant gains new powers, abilities and perceptions. At each new stage of development there are new accomplishments, mental and physical. The parents must know these steps in order to satisfy basic needs.

A baby at fifteen months is a different baby than he was at two months. At two months he was satisfied with milk as his sole food. At fifteen months he has teeth and fingers which have acquired some skill in holding a spoon. At fifteen months he needs different foods and methods of using his newly acquired skills in feeding himself to be happy and content. This same child at six months was content to play with his toes, but at twenty months he has wider interests and needs toys to keep him busy.

There are four different periods in the development of the infant:

1. The fetal period. 2. The neo-natal or newborn period. 3. The period between neo-natal and fifteen months of age and 4. The period from fifteen months to two years.

1. The fetal period: The unborn infant is in his most secure period of existence. He is safe, protected in his mother's womb and he does not have to exert any effort to survive. He has no problems to meet. He does not have to feed himself, and he is free from all annoyances.

2. The newborn period: This is the most trying period in the infant's life. The process of being born is a traumatic one. He is taken from a world of security and thrust into a world where from now on he has to be on his own. He has to breathe for himself, eat, sleep and eliminate on his own, if he is to survive.

It is most fortunate that the newborn baby works on an automatic basis. This helps to protect him through this dangerous and trying period. He has only one means of making known his wishes and that is to cry; and he cries often: when he is hungry, cold, wet, frightened and alone.

It is quite essential that at this period the parents should do all in their power to restore to the infant some semblance of the feeling of security he experienced in his prenatal days. During this period of new responsibility it is only good common sense to pay attention to the infant's cries and try to do something about satisfying his needs which he cannot do by himself.

This means feeding him when he is hungry, changing his diapers promptly, seeing that his crib is comfortable. This means picking him up when he cries and giving him rhythmic motion such as rocking and singing to him.

At this particular time we are dealing with a frightened, primitive human being who is finding himself in a wholly incomprehensible world with which he cannot cope. His only way of showing his needs is to cry. This situation calls for the gentlest and most understanding sort of care if he is to emerge from the newly born stage with any degree of confidence.

The infant at this stage will not be spoiled by attention. He cries not because he is contrary; he cries because he needs something. The parents' job is to find out what that something is. This kind of attention does not spoil him. It sets him off on the right foot in adjusting himself to his new world.

The best foundation for mental health is to establish in the infant's mind at the earliest possible age, the unfailing attention of his parents. To accomplish this, fondling, lullabies and rocking should be a part of the baby's life from the start. Later on, he will sense this affection in many other ways. This bond of affection becomes doubly important when later on, disciplinary measures become a part of the rearing of a normal child.

3. Newborn to fifteen months of age: At about eight weeks of age the baby's brain begins to take over control and the infant has the beginnings of voluntary activity. This is a process which takes several months and reaches significant stages at about fifteen months when he is able to stand and walk.

During this period the baby's growth is rather rapid. He is adjusting to routines of eating and sleeping, of developing some efficiency with arm and hand, of beginning to master his bowel and bladder control, of learning to laugh and acquire some degree of social consciousness.

Good psychological care is essential at this stage. Let us examine some of these individually:

Eating: Good psychological feeding care means individualizing each baby, by finding the time for meals that best suits his needs. Many babies seem to have a three-hour feeding rhythm and will scream for an hour when put on a four-hour schedule. Insisting on a feeding routine that does not fit is asking for trouble, because it ignores a basic need.

Proper feeding care also means allowing the baby to develop an appetite instead of forcing him to eat, giving him a chance to feed himself as soon as he is able, and respecting his preferences in diet. If he does not like one type of food, why not try one that he likes?

Sleeping: A sound psychological approach to sleep habits is to realize that sleep need never be taught to young babies. They spend most of their time asleep. As they grow older and acquire new abilities such as talking, using their hands, smiling, there is a purpose in being awake and sleep becomes of value as a means only of acquiring necessary rest.

To get the baby to sleep means to provide adequate sleeping opportunities and the sort of daily regime that gives him a chance to get tired. Sleep should never be a disciplinary agent. It should be enjoyed because it affords rest and recuperation, and should not be made a means of punishment.

Bowel-Control: No premature attempts at bowel training should be made. This will be a waste of time. Training should be initiated when the baby is able to sit up alone and can understand something of what is required of him and has settled down into a rhythm that makes it easy for his mother to know exactly when his daily bowel movement will naturally take place.

In most cases this will not take place until the infant is from six to eight months old. Urinary control, which is a much more complicated process for the baby to comprehend, should not be attempted until he is old enough to run about the house.

Nerve and muscle development: During the first fifteen months, the development of large muscles makes its most rapid progress. The baby learns to sit up, to crawl, to stand, to walk, to handle his rattle, his cup, his spoon, to play actively with toys and sometimes to feed himself. He must have enough freedom to practice and work at these new skills, if his muscular needs are to be met and psychological upheavals to be avoided.

4. Fifteen months to two years: During this period there is improvement in coordination of the fine muscles that leads to ceaseless hand and finger exploration. He becomes very active and is making a nuisance of himself. He is upsetting things, breaking vases and ruining furniture.

Although this is the time when the need to touch and handle should be met, in reality it is the time when parents too often begin with gusto to try to prevent growth and to make their children meet the standards of a complicated household. This training is quite often given in a conscientious spirit. Without adequate understanding of a child's needs, too many people expect adult behavior before a child is ready for it.

Instead of clamping down, it would be more to the purpose to get all the information available about appropriate toys and opportunities for safe and constructive play. The infant's mental health is promoted by wise and informed parents who know how to lessen frustrations and let the child have his way within reasonable limits.

For all human beings being loved is a prime necessity from the very beginning. The baby must be loved in order to be able to develop physically without setbacks and emotionally without developing any crippling neurotic traits and tendencies. Life without love for the infant is a life in which all normal tendencies for self-expression and mental development are thwarted.

The child needs love even more than the adult because it is more helpless and more plastic. Only by experiencing love can a child learn what love is and knowing love, return it and experience emotional satisfaction. When the child has little love, he has of necessity to turn his love to himself. When this is the case he cannot acquire the habit of giving love to others, a socializing bond to his environment which is so important for his proper emotional development.

A loveless child cannot form normal love relationships. He learns to use his parents for selfish ends. He has some degree of relatedness with his parents, but he does not love them. Whatever little love he has is frozen within himself. If this state of affairs persists he will endure more and more frustrations, and the time will come when the child will say that he does not want anything to do with his parents, because effective relationship without love is impossible. Love is an absolute requirement for all infants and children in order that they may grow up to be happily adjusted, neurotic-free adults.

The second stage in the growing up experiences of the child is the period from two to three years. The infant becomes somewhat aware of his environment. He begins to investigate and explore. He acquires some inkling of his role as a human being, and he begins to strive for independence and mastery. He becomes more aggressive in his actions and he begins to assert himself. Also at this time there is a development of social outlets for his aggressions. At this time he requires habit training which should not be too lax or too severe, particularly as regards toilet needs. A mistake is often made at this time by interference with the infant's independence and attempts at mastery, either in the form of rejection or over-protection. There should be neither severe restrictions nor too much yielding to the infant's demands. The child at this age, if frustrated, manifests anxieties, abnormal fears and compulsions. He may react with his stomach in the form of feeding difficulties, diarrhea and constipation. He may react with his bladder in the form of bed-wetting. He may also react with speech difficulties such as stuttering and stammering. Even at this stage the maladjusted child may exhibit character disorders, such as rage reactions, withdrawing from everyday realities or becoming excessively dependent upon others.

The next period is from three to six years. At this time the child has become a more social creature and there is need for contact with others than the immediate family. He learns about co-operative play. At this time there is also a keen interest in genital differences and the mystery of birth. He also has new problems to solve. At this time he enters nursery school or kindergarten. He has to learn to live with others of his age. He begins to see a widened horizon. If he has not been able to effect a good adjustment to his new environment he has new anxieties and conflicts to face. He may also exhibit psychosomatic disorders, such as stomach upsets, speech defects, skin irritations. There may be character disorders, such as lack of obedience, wilful destructiveness, sadistic tendencies. These require careful handling and correction.

The latency period is the next stage in the development of the child. This is the period from six to ten years of age. At this stage there is a need for further intellectual growth and understanding. There is need for further social contact and for organized team play. Particularly does he need to belong to a group. He has further problems to cope with. These relate to entry into grade school. He has to become more independent. He is also subjected to neighborhood stresses and conflicts. He may be exposed to racial and religious prejudices. To these he may react with various anxieties and tensions. He may exhibit tics, muscle spasms, nail-biting, masturbation, bed-wetting. He may have various character disorders, such as stealing, lying, sadistic and destructive behavior. Very careful supervision on the part of the parents is essential at this stage.

The child from six to ten lives in a world which is entirely different from the adult's. His world is a mixture of reality and sheer magic. He lives between fantasy and reality. He forms all sorts of fantastic notions and ideas about things around him and checks them against the ideas of other children, and finally of adults. He discards many of these ideas, but it is amazing how many fantastic ideas the child retains.

The child from six to ten lives in a world of magic and feels himself mixed up with magic, and it seems to him that certain things take place because he himself wills them to happen. Children believe in some internal vital force which has some relation to them and resides in all objects. They personify inanimate objects. This is entirely normal.

Puberty is an explosive stage in the child's development and includes the years from ten to fifteen. There is an awakening at this time of sexual feelings and interests for which a social outlet is necessary. Recreational programs, dancing, sports form satisfactory outlets for these tendencies. There is also the need to practice skills for successful participation in groups. At this time there is also a conflict between need for and defiance of parents. There is also a conflict in relation to sexual demands and social restrictions. There are also new anxieties and inner tensions to cope with.

Adolescence is the period between fifteen and twenty years. At this time there occurs a gradual emancipation from the control of the parents. The need arises to make a choice for one's life work. There is a growing sense of responsibility. Thoughts of courtship and marriage are uppermost. Sexual conflicts continue. There is also a conflict between dependence and independence. The more mature grow in independence. There are also new sources of inner conflicts and perplexities, and the more mature are able to resolve these without too much trouble.

Growing up is a period of joys and tribulations, of pleasures and anxieties, of physical, emotional and mental maturation. The child in becoming an adult has to exert physical and mental effort, acquire new experiences, face many problems and solve them. When these are accomplished, he has laid the foundations for a happy and successful way of living.

CHAPTER TWO

The Child as a
Functional Unit

The child is a socio-biological, body-mind unit. In previous times and sometimes even today, the body was thought to exist as a separate entity, as was also the mind. There were materialists who denied that the mind existed, and there were idealists who maintained that only the mind was real. Somewhat later there were the interactionists who stated that both existed, but they could not come to any agreement as to how they interacted each on the other. The modern conception is that the mind and body exist as a unit and not as separate entities. The mind acts on the body, and the body acts on the mind.

All disease, whether mental or physical, is regarded as an interplay between the individual and his environment. In some cases the surroundings are all-important, for if the body is infected with tuberculosis, the disease will almost invariably develop. In other cases, although the germ is present, the disease does not necessarily develop, as in diphtheria or typhoid. In such a case other factors will influence the result—the physical resistance of the body, whether the individual is otherwise healthy, whether he is happy or whether he seeks escape from difficulty by falling ill.

The environment means not only food and shelter, but happiness and other emotional factors as well. Neurosis is a conflict with the environment, sometimes with a situation which is really difficult, sometimes because the hereditary factor has made the child unable to cope with his troubles, and sometimes because of faulty upbringing which has made him react in the wrong way. All disease must be looked upon as a total reaction, both bodily and mentally to the environment.

This means very definitely that the body and mind cannot be separated. Mind does not exist in the body as an independent entity—like a tenant in a house. It is a process that goes on in living matter. The mind is the awareness of processes going on in the body.

A child functions as a whole. He responds to all situations as a total personality, not as a mind or as a body. The meaning of life is peculiarly personal and is individual in results as related to personal and social reactions. A child is in his environment and his environment is in him. He reacts with what he is to what he is not—which makes him other than he was. He matures physically and emotionally by this process. A child is active constantly in all planes. He attempts to mould his world and he resists being moulded by it.

A child also responds to stress, accident and disease as a body-mind unit. Whatever affects his body affects his mind and emotions, and whatever affects his mind and emotions certainly affects his body. Starvation, fever, thirst, accidents, pneumonia, bodily malformations, diabetes, heart disease give rise to disturbances in the mind as well as in the body. In the same way, anxiety, fear, jealousy, anger, worry, hatred may give rise, in time, to actual physical changes in the heart, the stomach, the lungs and in other vital organs. A feeling of disgust may result in nausea and vomiting. The peristaltic movements in the intestines are reversed in direction and this is accompanied by congestion of the blood vessels supplying the intestines and stomach. With frequent repetition, the lining of the intestines and stomach undergoes alteration and ulceration may follow. This may at first be temporary, but if the stress is imposed very frequently, these changes will become permanent.

Emotions and thought processes are never merely psychic, for the psyche is not something that exists somewhere in space; it is an organic agent. Neither does an organic disease remain wholly organic. It goes to the very core of the personality. Processes that are purely organic do not exist, for the body is fundamentally a psychophysical entity.

Mental and emotional conflict become intelligible only in relation to personal and social development in the presence of a communal culture. Social maladjustment is the expression of the conflict of the individual with the cultural pattern as it exists objectively in his social environment.

A child's survival depends upon his fitness to survive. Fitness is adjustment to his external and internal environment and health; unfitness is maladjustment and disease. Invalidism and emotional instability find their meaning in the struggle for existence. Disease and accident are not merely matters of the body, but also of the mind. A child may respond to these in a variety of ways.

No one actually knows where physical and mental reactions begin and end. Grief and gaiety, love and hatred, jealousy and contentment, failure and success, disappointment and surprise are not mere states of feelings, but states of being. They involve the heart and lungs, the stomach, the brain and the nerves. They are essentially total responses.

A cramp in the stomach may give rise to a fear of eating—a fear of eating may lead to the pain of hunger. Laughter arises from a sense of the incongruous or from an organic disturbance of the power inhibiting the laughter center of the brain. Symptoms of disease represent not only the disease process, but also the reaction of the personality afflicted by the physical condition. The reactions of fear or rage, despair, jealousy, hatred, wanting to love and fearing to love are psychosomatic and affect the power and the will to get well.

A child's utility lies in his capacity to function on physical, intellectual, emotional, social and spiritual planes. Limitations may exist upon any one plane and impair progress upon the other planes, or deficiencies in total organization may impede development upon any or all of the planes.

Mental health has been defined as personal adjustment to one's self and the world, with a maximum of personal and social effectiveness and satisfactions. The element of social responsibility is of definite importance. Social control is requisite for mental health.

Complete isolation of human actions is impossible. Individual behaviors affect social behaviors; social behaviors influence individual behaviors. The human machine is not a thing and inclusive in itself. It exists in close relationship to the industrial machine, the economic machine, the social machine. They all work in unison to fashion the world in which we live.

A child cannot exist by himself. He exists in close relatedness with other people and with his surroundings. A child's existence is not enclosed in the boundaries of his physical body. In his actions, feelings, intentions, thoughts, memories, the child reaches beyond himself into the surrounding world, and the world reaches into his existence.

It is quite definite that the child is a socio-biological body-mind unit who lives in close relatedness with all other living creatures in the world around him. A child cannot live in himself and by himself. He cannot be isolated and insulated against his environment. His actions affect everyone and everything around him. In the same way the world's actions constantly impinge upon him and he reacts to these influences as a body-mind unit. His happiness, his emotional stability, his health, his effectiveness as a human being depend to a great extent on how he reacts to these influences. His sense of inner harmony is dependent largely upon his capacities to react to the stresses of his external and internal environments.

CHAPTER THREE

What Causes Jealousy

As we are to discuss the jealous child, it is necessary to gain some idea as to what jealousy is, what causes it and what can be done about it.

Jealousy is an emotion. What is an emotion? Essentially it is a state of intense feeling. An emotion has a definite physiological purpose. It tends to keep the body from losing its equilibrium during stress. An emotion is the result of certain common environmental situations. In other words, an emotion is a feeling aroused by stressful situations.

An emotion is a meaningful performance. It is mobilized in certain situations for definite purposes. While experiencing an emotion we live in another world—in a world where things are pleasanter. This is one of the purposes of an emotion—to save the individual in an unstable situation.

Emotions are part and parcel of behavior. Behavior is determined by the trend towards self-realization. There is always a tendency toward the best possible adjustment of the personality and the world in which the individual has to live. The difficulties encountered—the inner conflicts—produce different kinds of reactions. These reactions produce different emotions. The individual brings himself into these emotional conditions because they make for better self-realization. Thus no action occurs without emotion.

In everyday life various conditions arise which more or less facilitate action. The human being assumes and has to assume different attitudes in order to realize all his capacities. The role played by the emotions differs with these different attitudes. Emotions are a deliberate means to coming to terms with particular situations. Thus emotions are always purposeful.

Jealousy is an emotion which is constantly experienced by all human beings. It is as much a part of human nature as is anger or fear or love. Jealousy has its origin in fear or uncertainty. It arises from a feeling of being rejected or neglected or unappreciated. It is a most uncomfortable and plaguing feeling which takes its roots in a loss of self-esteem.

Jealousy is not limited to any particular period in life; it appears all through life. Jealousy is the source of unbridled hatred in children as well as in adults. There is no doubt about the role that jealousy plays between brothers and sisters. Jealousy of one or the other parent in neurotic children is a very real and devastating experience. Such an attitude may have a lasting influence in later life and give rise to all sorts of neurotic ills.

Excessive jealousy is often thought to be conditioned by jealousy experienced in childhood toward a brother or sister or one of the parents. Brother or sister jealousy as it occurs among healthy children, jealousy toward a newborn baby, for example, vanishes without leaving a scar as soon as the child feels sure that he does not lose any of the love or attention he has had hitherto. Excessive jealousy which is never overcome in children is due to neurotic conditions.

Jealousy arises in cases in which a child feels neglected and discriminated against because of various conditions such as physical deformity, social status, economic conditions, chronic disease, racial and national origin, etc. Jealousy arises in a child who lacks something that he would very much like to possess. This may be a perfect body, normal health, social position, economic security, parents who are esteemed by the community, etc.

Jealousy as an emotion leads to other emotional states. It results in envy which is closely akin to jealousy. Envy results when we want something that someone else has which we lack. Thus the jealous child is also an envious child. A deformed child is jealous of a physically perfect child and envies him; he, too, would like to have a perfect body. The same is true of the diabetic child who envies the healthy child and is jealous of him. This is also true of the impoverished child who is jealous of the child whose parents are wealthy.

The jealous child is not only an envious child, but a frustrated one as well. He is frustrated because he cannot attain what he lacks, or because he feels that he cannot attain what he should. The child with a harelip is jealous of the one who is perfect, is envious of the child without a harelip because he would like to have a perfect lip himself, and is frustrated because no efforts have been made to repair his defect.

The sum total result of jealousy, envy and frustration in the child is, in mild cases, unhappiness, and in more severe cases, a neurosis. A neurosis is an inadequate, unsuccessful attempt to restore the emotional equilibrium disturbed by the presence of unsatisfied or poorly satisfied subjective urges. These subjective urges, in the jealous child, are of different kinds. They may be those due to poor health, physical defects, feelings of inferiority due to social and economic status, etc.

There is quite a great deal that can be done to alleviate the tensions and conflicts in the jealous child. Each situation which gives rise to this emotion is quite specific, and each situation has to be considered individually in all its aspects. This is the object of the present book.

In the chapters which follow the dynamics of jealousy will be considered in various situations (physical, health, racial, social, economic, etc.) . Also to be treated will be the methods that are available to modify these situations so as to relieve the feeling of jealousy and restore the emotional equilibrium of the child. At the present time a great deal can be done to make the jealous child a happy child.

CHAPTER FOUR

How the Child Reacts to
His Physical Defects

Any kind of physical defect is a definite mental hazard. Unfortunately the human body is subjected to many accidents and quite often a more or less permanent defect is the result. In childhood the most common physical defects are harelip, cleft palate, facial birthmarks, saddle nose, hunch back, webbed fingers, cross-eyes, disfiguring scars, crooked teeth and contractures resulting from burns. Many of these defects are those with which the child is born, and others are acquired during childhood.

Facial disfigurement of one kind or another is quite common. This disfigurement may be in the form of a too prominent nose, a hooked nose, or other nasal defect, or it may be a harelip, a large mole on the cheek or other blemish which attracts unfavorable attention.

The most common facial cosmetic defect is a nose that is either too large, too bulbous, hooked, or in other ways deformed. The nose is the most conspicuous feature of the face and any deviation from the usual is immediately apparent. If it is not normal it becomes the target of jests and ridicule, and upon the ability of its possessor to take these jests and disregard them depends his peace of mind.

However, most children with a nasal defect are sensitive. They quite often believe that others look down upon them because of the quite unusual shape of their nose. They become shy and sensitive and quite often suffer from considerable anxiety. As they grow older they go through all sorts of maneuvers to avoid presenting their face in its most unfavorable view—usually the profile. They sometimes develop peculiar mannerisms with their hands, for the express purpose of hiding their nose. They tend to keep in the background as much as possible.

It is quite true that such children become suspicious and almost paranoid in their thoughts. They begin to believe that everybody they meet concentrates his attention upon their nose. They have an uncomfortable and devastating feeling that they are being constantly observed and inwardly ridiculed because of their facial blemish. Because of this they do not join in play with other children.

Children suffering from a nasal or other quite noticeable facial disfigurement are constricted in their bodily movements, in their flow of attention, and in their inability to react warmly to other children. Quite often such children become badly adjusted to their disfigurement and are constantly suffering from a feeling that other children are more interested in their physical defect than in them.

Facial disfigurement quite often results in a feeling of inferiority which persists as long as the disfigurement remains. Quite often such children seclude themselves and alter their desires and emotions and activities because of their facial appearance.

There is little doubt that the teeth of a child have a great deal to do with how he behaves, feels and acts. Sound teeth, clean teeth, pearly-white teeth and well-shaped teeth add a great deal to a child's personal appearance. The consciousness of dental health and beauty makes a child feel good and act properly. Deformed teeth, painful teeth, brownish, scaly teeth certainly give a child a feeling of inferiority and unworthiness.

Dental health affects personality very markedly, and even pain of dental origin is manifested physically, mentally and emotionally and socially, either singly, or, as is more usual, in combination. When a child has a toothache there is frequently fever. But even when fever is absent one notes a loss of appetite, enlarged glands, insomnia, petulance, crying and perhaps convulsions. Older children manifest diminished attention, lack of concentration, reduced interest in school activities and in play activities. Some may show tendencies toward over-activity or marked depressions, even to the point of complete withdrawal from all activities.

Poor position of the teeth in children very often gives rise to various behavior problems. It hardly matters what the type of malposition may be, one is apt to find behavior disturbances because of this. Some of the behavior problems due to dental malposition which have been observed are: tics of the head and neck, choreiform movements, marked fatigue and a general lack of interest. Occasionally, one notes tantrums, lack of self-control, pugnacity, depression and disagreeableness in social relationships.

Impacted teeth also show their effect on behavior, quite often because of the pain. Under such conditions there is often lessened attention, disinclination to study, impaired memory, distractibility and poor scholastic showing. The impaction results in an accentuation of previously existent emotional trends and peculiarities.

Absorption of toxic material is mainly the result of dental caries. The fact that learning difficulties result from caries in childhood is not widely appreciated. It has been estimated that more than 10 per cent of the loss of school progress is incidental to dental caries with its consequent absence from school and mental distraction. A child may have a high degree of intelligence but suffer from dental caries with subsequent diminished attention, concentration and available energy to such a degree that his school work will suffer markedly with failure in most of his subjects.

There are many emotional disorders which may result,

depending upon the amount of toxic material that has been absorbed. Thus fear may be accentuated, anxieties increased, irritability and peevishness multiplied. It has been observed that as a result of toxic absorption from diseased teeth there may arise quite a variety of social disturbances in children, not only in poor social relationships, poor school work, but frequently in irritability, intractability, disobedience, revolt against authority and truancy.

The problem of dental deformities generally falls into three different groups: congenital, developmental and acquired. The reaction to personal appearance is varied, but needless to say, many sensitive children are made self-conscious and unhappy by such avoidable deformity. Behavior disturbances which often result are stubbornness, pugnacity, delinquency and nervousness. In many instances the dental deformity is responsible for difficulties in speech function, because so many of the sounds are dependent upon a proper approximation of the teeth and coordination of the tongue, lips and teeth.

Occasionally, one notes a relationship between dental development and delinquency, particularly when there is irritation and stimulation to escape pain, or when ideas of revenge for personal distress arise, or after the development of a state of unreasonableness due to chronic suffering. There is no doubt that dental abnormalities tend to undermine emotional stability.

A child's personal relation to his teeth and the relation of his teeth to his social behavior are the basis of some of his behavior and reactions. Sound teeth often go not only with sound physical health, but sound mental and emotional health. Particularly in childhood is adequate dental care of the utmost importance. Only proper dental care, eliminating dental deformities and defects, can in these cases prevent behavior disturbances during childhood.

The first and foremost mental and emotional effect of any

deformity is that of shame and a feeling of inferiority. Children are very observant of the strange and unusual. Because of their unsophistication and very natural curiosity, they are very apt to pay undue and rather disconcerting attention to any defect or abnormality in a playmate. A child has no inhibitions, and naturally he does not make any attempt to conceal his curiosity or refrain from making a remark about a defect publicly, or ridiculing his companion who is a little out of the ordinary. His intentions may be sympathetic or frankly malicious, and he is most likely to be openly frank in his discussions and opinions. In a less purposeful manner, he will shun the deformed playmate or will force him into an inferior social position. Quite often a note of permanence is added to these childhood stigmas by "dubbing" the deformed child with a nickname that refers to his defect.

Little wonder it is then that the great majority of deformed children quickly develop a feeling of inferiority and a sense of shame. Probably this mental factor develops much earlier than is generally supposed. As the child matures he becomes increasingly more sensitive. This inferiority complex does not usually become a serious problem until the child enters school. He is then brought to realize his difference from the others, and he is not able to acquire the intimate companionships enjoyed by his playmates. When adolescence is reached, a sense of despair and a pessimistic philosophy of life admixed with all sorts of peculiar personality traits have been established.

Personality depends on two fundamental drives. The one is for self-expression and the other for conformance with accepted social standards. When these two factors coincide, a pleasing personality develops. When this is applied to the deformed, the result is obvious. The deformed child may have every mental and physical faculty for self-expression possessed by other children, but, because of his deformity, he is either restrained by others or avoids the personal contacts necessary for such expression. Activities are either shunned or altered.

Because of this rather unfortunate situation three reactions may result: First, the child may succumb to these obstacles and accept non-expression as his lot. He may withdraw within himself, become seclusive, shy and avoid giving play to his instinctual drives. Second, the child may develop a compensatory over-abundance of self-expression to satisfy his injured ego. He will become over-active, overdo things, and in general make a pest and nuisance of himself in an attempt to draw attention away from his defect. Third, under fortunate circumstances the deformed child may replace the suppressed modes of self-expression with alternative ones of equal merit. He will find other ways and means of expressing his skills and abilities which his defect may prevent or inhibit. This last reaction is the most satisfactory one.

A second important factor in the development of personality is the acquisition of popularity. Before a handicapped child can gain recognition of the group, he must overcome the tendency of other children to maintain the natural impression of abnormality and undesirability. Many unfortunates are inclined to give in to these difficulties and to make no effort to become one of the group. Others become resentful toward their obstacles and mistreatment. Blame for their failures is either inwardly or openly placed on all manner of circumstances and people. These are the children who may develop objectionable social behavior, since they often cannot obtain desirable employment, may not succeed in matrimonial ventures, and will not maintain friendships. As a result, they may often resort to criminal activities.

Perhaps the dominant emotion of children suffering from physical defects is that of jealousy, regretful of not being physically whole and sound like other children. They suffer from a sense of deprivation. They feel they have been cheated out of a normal body they should have had. For this reason they are chronically jealous of other children who have no physical defects. Some may adjust to this state of affairs, others become bitter and resentful.

The methods used to overcome these mental traits in children are those that aim at overcoming the physical defects. First is the method of prevention. As far as congenital defects are concerned, little or nothing can be done in the way of prevention. Acquired defects, on the other hand, are preventable.

The second method is that of the earliest possible correction. When a deformity of any type or severity is present, the most important single item in the avoidance of undesirable personality changes is the most complete surgical restoration at the earliest possible date that is feasible. This is a hard and fast rule, and there are no exceptions to it.

It is of the greatest importance to have deformities corrected, if possible, before the child enters school. This is the age of greatest mental and social reaction to deformity, from which every effort should be made to protect the child. Fortunately, there are but a few conditions in which at least a partial restoration cannot be made during the first five years of life.

Surgical correction in early childhood is the most valuable method of preventing undesirable personality traits. Unfortunately, early correction of the deformity in some instances is impossible; in others it is not possible to obtain perfect cosmetic results. Therefore, a special program of training must be embarked upon. This is the sort of training that might be used for any normal child, with emphasis on certain aspects which are most important for the deformed child.

First, the deformed child must be taught to anticipate difficulties and acquire a sense of self-reliance. Every effort should be directed toward not allowing the child to become spoiled. The training must begin as soon as the child is born by not responding with a burst of attention every time the baby cries or frets. As the child grows older the same principles should be continued.

Since the deformed child is probably destined for one or more operations with some degree of pain, he should be thoroughly prepared for the ordeal. He should not be cajoled into the physician's office dishonestly by being told that it will not hurt. He should be made to understand that he may be hurt and should at all times be told by both the physician and his parents exactly what to expect.

The handicapped child is most likely to be deprived of many things commonly sought after for their supposed value, such as money, friends, esteem, beauty, amusements and romance. Unless such children understand that, regardless of group standards in this respect, true value depends entirely upon the enjoyment they themselves derive, they are apt to do many useless, foolhardy and even dishonest things to attain their desires, especially for friendship.

Parents of a handicapped child should make every effort to help him readjust his sense of values. Above all, he must learn that true friendship exists only in those who like him in spite of his deformity, irrespective of his possessions or ability to do something to buy their favor.

Speech training is called for in children with cleft palate. Gymnastics are important for children with bone defects and deformities. Cross eyes are greatly improved by exercises to develop the use of the eye muscles. Another important part in the training of handicapped children is that directed toward feasible modes of self-expression, and, later in life, toward trades and professions which will not be hindered by the deformity. To be successful, this training must follow the child's own interests and talents and should never be forced or predetermined by parents or teachers. Constructive hobbies which keep the child happily occupied in his spare time are of the greatest value. Special training in art, music, athletics, handicrafts and the like should be made available whenever possible.

Whatever type of compensatory education can be worked out, if the child finds one or more satisfying methods of self-expression which keep him happily occupied and which receive recognition from others, that child will develop along essentially normal lines, regardless of his deformity.

In addition, there are a few simple things that you can teach your child to help him attain a sense of social usefulness:

1. Have the child regard himself as an individual of some importance, a useful member of society, whose opinions and thoughts count for something.

2. Teach your child that there is no place in his scheme of things for a sense of futility and uselessness. Everyone is of some use in this world.

3. Teach your child to acquire a sense of self-confidence and self-esteem. There is hardly a situation in life to be jealous about, if he is self-confident, and if he has a staunch belief in his own good personal qualities.

4. Teach him to acquire a sense of self-detachment. Teach him to view the situation from afar, and it will not seem so terribly overwhelming after all.

5. Teach your child to develop a sense of humor and to learn to laugh at himself.

6. Teach your child not to be fearful and self-conscious when he meets people.

7. Teach him to be his own good self, not to try to imitate others. He has his own good points which should be emphasized.

The principal object in dealing with the physically handicapped child is to have him become adjusted to his condition, to impart to him the ability to live within the limits imposed by bodily equipment, and to do this without a sense of futility and despair.

CHAPTER FIVE

The Psychological Difficulties of the Child
With Rheumatic Heart Disease

Rheumatic fever is, tragically enough, an altogether too common childhood ailment. While in its active stages the disease causes considerable discomfort, pain and distress, its after-effects on the child's way of living are considerably more serious.

Rheumatic fever may come on insidiously or its onset may be quite sudden. When the disease has an insidious onset, the child always shows signs of feeling quite ill and irritable for several days or even weeks before the more definite symptoms of the disease develop. The disease may also come on rather suddenly following or during a cold. During the acute stages of the disease the child is quite ill, often experiencing considerable pain in the swollen joints. The most serious thing about rheumatic fever is that it very often affects the heart, and it is for this reason that great care must be taken in the acute phases of rheumatic fever.

Of necessity the child must remain in bed for quite a long period of time, and even after the bed rest is discontinued, the child cannot resume a normal life. His activity must be quite severely restricted and limited lest the heart become affected. Even under the most favorable circumstances, he must, for many years thereafter, lead a sedentary life with all its annoyances, irksomeness and emotional handicaps as far as a child is concerned.

The tragic thing about one attack of rheumatic fever is that it makes another attack more likely. One of the things that a child must avoid in order to prevent another attack of rheumatic fever is the common cold, for the cold has a tendency to develop into rheumatic fever with further damage to the heart. The child, therefore, must be carefully guarded against the common cold; he must be put to bed and his activities severely restricted at the least sign of a cold. This involves irksome limitation of his freedom, of his playing activities and ordinary physical exertion of any kind. This is very distasteful to any child, and in time he becomes emotionally upset. If the heart has been damaged, as it quite often is, the child must look forward to a life of limited activity. He cannot take part in the ordinary play and games of childhood. He must remain quiet during a period of his life when physical activity finds its greatest play and affords the most gratifying pleasures. He must learn to derive satisfaction from relatively sedentary activities, and this, for a child is extremely difficult and emotionally unsatisfactory.

In time the child whose ordinary, everyday activities must be restricted because of his heart condition begins to feel that he is in a class set apart from other children. He is a child but he cannot act like a child. He cannot be boisterous and active like other children. He must act quietly and sedately like grown-ups. He begins to have the feeling that there is something "queer" about him, and so, in fact, do other children.

It is little wonder that the great majority of children with rheumatic heart disease quickly develop a feeling of inferiority, a sense of shame, jealousy and envy of children who are able and permitted to lead a normally active life. Probably these mental factors develop much earlier than is generally supposed. As the child matures he may become increasingly more sensitive. The feeling of inferiority and "queerness" does not usually become a serious and pressing problem until the child enters school. It is then that he begins to realize that he is different from the others, and he is unable to acquire the intimate companionships enjoyed by his playmates. He is subjected to other uncomfortable feelings. He naturally becomes envious of those of his friends who are able to play baseball and football. He is plagued by jealousy because others possess something which he does not—a sound heart that does not restrict their playtime activities. Quite often feelings of jealousy are closely bound up with feelings of being hurt and lonely.

The handicapped child, such as one with a rheumatic heart, also becomes unduly sensitive. He is more or less constantly conscious of being set apart from other children. For this reason, he is unduly affected by the moods, opinions and actions of his playmates. What other children feel, think and do, or, just as important, what these children imagine that other children feel, think and do about them, is a constant source of painful annoyance under practically all circumstances.

The child with rheumatic heart disease constantly has a feeling of being insecure as well as vulnerable and touchy. Somehow these go together. He feels himself a misfit. He lives in fear, anticipates fear and reacts to it quite severely.

Another effect of rheumatic heart disease on the child's emotional life is on his capacity to deal with his problems aggressively. The normal child is able to deal with most of his problems in a normal aggressive manner and in this way he is able to protect himself. The normal child expresses his aggressiveness in physical activity, quite often vigorous physical activity. The child with rheumatic heart disease is not able to do this. He must avoid all expression of aggressiveness because this is dangerous to his well-being, indeed to his life itself.

The child with rheumatic heart disease can be helped considerably by his parents to lead a normal, well-adjusted life.

The sick child depends upon his parents for training and guidance even more so than upon others, such as his teachers or companions. His parents' opinions and points of view become his by close contact and association.

There are a few practical suggestions which parents of children with rheumatic heart disease should always keep in mind:

1. Teach your child to anticipate difficulties in the course of daily living and to acquire a sense of self-reliance.

2. Do not spoil and over-protect your child because of his illness. This only serves to make him more conscious of his handicap and increases his sense of shame and envy.

3. Teach your child that true friendship exists only in those who like him for himself alone in spite of his handicap and inability to join other children in physical activity.

4. Always give your child a reason for the command laid down upon him. By understanding the reason for an order, such as not playing too vigorously or joining in very active sports, he will be able to govern himself more intelligently and more willingly.

5. Always allow him to discuss his plans, problems and pleasures with you. By doing so he will acquire a greater sense of security and personal self-esteem. This will help him considerably to overcome his feelings of inferiority, envy and jealousy.

6. Teach him that when he is not able to indulge in physical activity he can derive just as much pleasure from sedentary occupations, such as reading, writing, collecting stamps and coins, and by intellectual achievement. It is much more gratifying to develop the mind than to acquire bulging muscles.

7. Acquaint him with the fact that handicapped persons can and do achieve high positions in life. The story of Franklin D. Roosevelt who achieved his greatest potentialities while a victim of polio should prove an inspiration

to him. There are a great many others: Steinmetz, Helen Keller, Alec Templeton, among many others, though severely handicapped, were able to do great work, lead happy lives and achieve great personal satisfaction.

8. Always have a little praise for your child and encourage his efforts, no matter how ineffectual they may seem. Praise is always an incentive to do good work and quite often to do better work, in spite of any handicap.

9. Always make sure your child knows that you appreciate and love him. Demonstrate this in ways he can understand. In this way he will become less conscious of his handicap and acquire greater confidence.

10. Do not show pity or concern about his condition. He will sense this and become even more aware of his handicap and more discouraged with himself. Treat him like you do others, like an ordinary, normal child, and not one who must always be protected and guarded constantly. This will help to re-establish a feeling of being normal like the others and tend to dissipate any feelings of self-pity and frustration.

CHAPTER SIX

The Tuberculous Child's
Mental Outlook

Tuberculosis in childhood is an ailment which brings with it not only definite changes in the lungs but in the child's mental and emotional outlook as well. Like any chronic ailment its effects are prolonged and influence the entire perspective of the child which almost always calls for marked modifications in his way of life.

Tuberculosis begins as an acute ailment which in time becomes chronic and disabling. It is a serious disease with many threatening aspects. The word tuberculosis to the child connotes danger and disaster, and for this reason very often results in a state of intense anxiety. He is often preoccupied with thoughts of death. In many cases there is a tendency to suffer from insomnia because there is a fear of dying while asleep. Tuberculosis is regarded as a hopeless disease in the child's mind and it is associated with an early death.

Because the child is constantly preoccupied with thoughts of death, there is a marked tendency to deny that death is a reality. Torn between the realization that death is real and the wish that it is not, the child often experiences feelings of depression. His usual mood is one of discouragement.

The usual response to danger in any form is increased physical activity—an attempt to run away from danger. The tuberculous child is restricted in his activity because of his ailment. The essential part of his treatment is rest—enforced rest. He cannot indulge in the normal activity of other children. He must therefore obtain relief in fantasy. This fantasy takes the form in which he sees himself in constant motion—running, roller skating, baseball, skipping rope, dancing. There is a marked tendency to dramatize this fantasy. He sees himself a personage of heroic physical proportions with remarkable physical prowess. This serves to produce severe conflict, for he knows that he must rest, always rest and be quiet, since any sort of activity has a tendency to prolong his illness and spread the disease.

Because the tuberculous child has the feeling that he is constantly in danger he is always aware of all sorts of aggressive and threatening figures—ghosts, robbers, murderers, giants, witches, etc. The very environment is full of aggressive forces which he is constantly up against. To counteract these he resorts to wishful thinking, refusal to face the reality of his situation, denying that he is really as sick as he actually is.

Because he is rather severely handicapped by his disease, the tuberculous child has a marked feeling of inadequacy, insufficiency and helplessness. His unwillingness to treat his problem realistically in time has repercussions on his reactions in general. He becomes vague and fuzzy about a great many things and is indefinite in his concepts of many quite ordinary things.

The child sick with tuberculosis suffers in his interpersonal relationships. He has limited emotional contact with others, and there appears to be no real desire for emotional exchange. He is emotionally insulated; he lives in an emotional vacuum. He is constantly seeking for support and reassurance from those about him. This is so because he is not able to maintain simple daily routines, for these are constantly being threatened by his ailment.

The tuberculous child finds himself living in an unfriendly world—a world which is kind and protective to other children, but not to him. The world outside is full of strange, forbidding, dangerous and threatening forces. He feels different and apart from other children; other children may play, have fun, go to school, move about freely, have plans for the future. He cannot do these things. He has a desolate feeling that everyone and everything is against him. He begins to experience feelings of shame, inferiority, envy and jealousy. He sorely lacks what other children have. Jealousy becomes an outstanding emotion because of his deprivations. He is jealous of what he does not have.

Many tuberculous children feel that their parents have rejected them. They feel isolated from the world outside and rejected inwardly because they cannot play with other children and cannot react with their normal instincts to everyday, ordinary situations.

In any prolonged, confining and anxiety-generating illness there is a tendency toward regression—going back to a more pleasant stage in life. For this reason many tuberculous children are not as mature as normal children—they tend to be more infantile and dependent in their behavior. However, in many instances, this is only of short duration. The tuberculous child tends to resist these regressive trends; he tends to avoid dependency and part of the difficulty in his management appears to be related to the drive to maintain independence. However, regressive tendencies are often found in the acute stages of tuberculosis and whenever anxiety is greatest.

One of the most irksome things to the child with tuberculosis arises from the fact that he must be isolated and subjected to all sorts of precautionary measures. This makes him feel like a pariah and outcast. He feels different and stigmatized; he becomes increasingly jealous of other children who are not subjected to these restrictions.

Quite a few tuberculous children have the feeling that tuberculosis is contracted through uncleanliness and for this reason is shameful and disgraceful. This naturally adds further impact to the psychic trauma. This results in resentment which often leads to neglect of precautions. The tuberculous child has the feeling that he is being wronged constantly and he responds with aggression and defiance of authority. He reacts in a markedly exaggerated way to any deprivation and criticism. In some instances the tuberculous child has quite marked feelings that the whole world is conspiring against him. This is, in part, a reaction to his illness.

The limitations of normal contacts, the feelings of stigma and isolation, and the fact that in many cases the disease has been contracted from parents and siblings lead to feelings of resentment against the source of their disease. They hate the individual from whom they contracted the disease and blame him for the extremely uncomfortable state they find themselves in.

The tuberculous child finds comfort in pretending that he is not ill; he derives some pleasure in identifying himself with the normal. He strives to attain a feeling of some degree of significance by minimizing his drawbacks.

The child ill with tuberculosis has a tendency to defeatism because of a potentially hostile and unfriendly world too unreliable and unfair to satisfy his needs for security. The problem of defeatism may be viewed as a potential way of life, a design for living, which is in keeping with the personal needs of the child, who has been overwhelmed and thwarted in his attempts to live a normal, active life. The child is not only reacting to a difficult situation but is actively contributing to it in a manner which leads to an increasing need for self-deception and a diminishing sense of self-esteem.

The tuberculous child should be encouraged to express himself and to realize his own importance. A pride in himself should be substituted for the previous sense of frustration about his illness. He can be taught to achieve inner feelings that spell satisfaction to his fundamental emotional needs.

The tuberculous child can be taught to realize that tuberculosis is not the dread disease he thinks it is. Many individuals with this disease have lived useful lives and have accomplished much in the way of personal achievement and in contributions to the welfare of mankind. Some of the greatest writers and scientists have had tuberculosis, and they were able to live useful lives because they learned to live with their disease. The sense of jealousy can be considerably lessened by making the child feel that his restrictions and deprivations are only of a temporary nature, and that in time he will be like others about him. Also, being sick has its compensations: he is learning to take better care of his body; he is given an opportunity to enrich his mental and emotional capacities in quiet activities which, in the long run, are the real values in human existence.

CHAPTER SEVEN

The Restricted World of
the Diabetic Child

Diabetes in children is, unfortunately, not too rare a condition. This disease has been found in children at all ages, but in general it is quite rare in the very young child. The causes of diabetes in children are not well understood. Heredity, of course, plays an important part, for its influence has been noted in about one third of the cases reported. In many cases the onset of diabetes is abrupt. It has been observed to occur with or after fevers and infections.

When diabetes occurs in children, it usually tends to be severe, for it occurs at a critical time of growth and development. The younger the child, the severer the diabetes is likely to be. There is one notable characteristic which differentiates juvenile diabetes from adult diabetes—there is no history of overweight. Instead there is a tendency to overheight.

Before the discovery of insulin, diabetes in children in most cases ended fatally. However, now with scientific methods of insulin treatment at our disposal, the diabetic child usually does quite well.

It has been noted that diabetes has a tendency to affect children of the higher economic classes. Children among the poor seem to be less subjected to this ailment. Dr. Duncan, a well known expert in juvenile diabetes, has gone so far as to say, "I have never known a newsboy who had diabetes." Rich food, overindulgence in carbohydrates, and lack of physical activity among the well-to-do seem to be contributory causes to the onset of juvenile diabetes.

The presence of diabetes in a child, in many instances, presents problems that seem overwhelming not only to the child but his family as well. Juvenile diabetes has a tendency towards greater severity. For this reason the child must be under constant supervision, his daily activities are curtailed and his way of life regimented.

The onset of diabetes in a child has a profound effect not only on the child but his family as well. The family's acceptance of the disease and the way in which the medical regime is followed is a good index of the family relationship. The initial reaction of the family to the knowledge that a child has diabetes is naturally one of great emotional disturbance and bewilderment. Some mothers are able to assimilate the upset and learn the necessary techniques of management more rapidly. Others seem to be in a state of bewildered shock for a longer period of time. The sooner the mother calms down and accepts the fact that the child has diabetes the sooner the child also tends to overcome his initial shock of learning that he must from now on lead a different sort of life.

In emotionally disturbed families poor cooperation becomes a focus of existing conflicts and is quite frequently associated with poor regulation of the child's activities. Co-operation, however, does not always mean an absence of neurotic conflicts. It may mean expressing a repressive, perfectionistic attitude toward the child. A more lenient medical regime would help such families accept diabetes with less guilt and anxiety, and so offer the child a better opportunity for normal personality development.

It has been found that socio-economic factors appear to play a more significant role in influencing behavior of juvenile diabetics than in the case of non-diabetic children. In those from superior home environments (in regard to both financial status and emotional stability) excellent or good adjustments to diabetes are made more readily than in children from poor home environments.

It goes without saying that how the parents react to the child's disease has a great deal to do with how the child will accept his disease. Parental reactions to the diabetic child may be one of two types—either over-solicitous coddling or one of resentment and rejection. When the child is over-protected by an over-anxious mother he develops into a passive, dependent, infantile type. When he is resented and rejected he becomes a belligerent personality. It occasionally happens that a child who initially cooperated with the first type of reaction will in time rebel against over-protection.

In addition to adjusting to parental reactions, the diabetic child has special problems in sibling relationships associated with special and restricted diet requirements. When he sees that his brothers and sisters are able to eat what they want and he is restricted in his diet he becomes jealous and resentful. He has not arrived at a stage in his thinking which can make exceptions in unusual cases. He cannot think of himself as an unusual case because he has diabetes. Being restricted to certain foods, he feels that he is in a class set apart, and he is envious and jealous of the members of his immediate family who can sit down to a meal with a variety of sweets which he must avoid.

Even when the attitude of the parents toward his illness is a healthy one, these children suffer insecurity in their social relationships because of the inability to participate fully in all active sports. This gives rise also to feelings of inadequacy and inferiority further mixed with jealousy and envy.

In general, diabetic children show great variations in their characteristic behavior and personality features. A few are happy, out-going and well-adjusted. Others suffer from various personality and behavior difficulties. Some become obsessive; they experience all sorts of unpleasant thoughts that intrude into their minds. Others become compulsive; they feel that they have to do certain things, like arranging their material in a certain way, step on the cracks on the sidewalk, practice their music at a certain hour, etc. These mannerisms serve in a way to reduce their inner tensions, which have been generated by their restricted activities. Some children, mostly those who have become diabetic at an early age, are unusually submissive. Some show depressive tendencies and rebelliousness.

With the approach of adolescence some children present outstanding behavior aberrations, most of them occurring in children who have had former problems in family adjustments. These behavior problems include bellicose acts, euphoria, wanderlust, depression and suicide trends.

In general, however, maturity has a favorable effect on even those children who suffered severe maladjustments during adolescence. Even those whose outlook appears rather hopeless do surprisingly well after leaving the retarding influence of a poor childhood environment.

Diabetes enforces a way of life to which a child and his family will react according to pre-existing yet unspecific patterns. In many cases diabetes has a tendency to reinforce existing problems.

Diabetic children have a strong tendency to be envious and jealous of other children who lead a normal, unregimented and unrestricted life. They feel in a class set apart. They feel rejected by others and they react to this rejection by rebellious behavior and bellicosity. They always have a chip on their shoulders and are always on the defensive.

What can the parent do to make the life of the diabetic child more meaningful and less stressful? He can:

1. Provide a good degree of stability and security.
2. Meet the child's essential needs and desires with appropriate outlets and satisfaction.

3. Provide facilities and freedom for the development, training and use of the child's potential strengths and for the overcoming and minimizing of remedial difficulties.

More specifically:

1. Teach your child not to take refuge in evasive procedures when something unpleasant is facing him. Teach him to face it squarely.

2. Teach him not to minimize his own just demands simply to avoid conflict and unpleasantness.

3. Teach him to meet just reproaches by not using evasive answers and explanations.

4. Teach him not to expect everyone to like or admire him.

5. Teach him that his illness is not a stigma or a disgrace, and that his way of life has certain advantages: it inculcates in him an ability to take care of his health in more specific ways than if he were not diabetic; it makes him aware of the importance of healthful living. Teach him that diabetes is not a hopeless disease and that he can live a normal life with it, and be happy and content, in spite of it.

CHAPTER EIGHT

The Emotional Difficulties
of the Obese Child

There are two very common feeding complaints that almost all parents have in regard to their children: they do not eat enough, or they eat too much. The child who eats too much does so for a very good reason. Dr. Hilde Bruch, who has done quite a bit of research on this problem, has said: "In some cases food seems to be the only source of satisfaction and the longing for it becomes an uncontrolled craving. An insecure and unloved child may be thwarted in developing creative sources of satisfaction and he may seek relief from his feelings of anxiety and helplessness by eating."

The overweight child is an unhappy, emotionally insecure child. He is so not because he wants to be so, but because of conditions beyond his control. He is a member of a family which is not normally adjusted. Most often his mother is of the domineering type while his father is unaggressive with little drive and no ambition. The parents are always at odds with each other. There are constant quarrels, disagreements and bickerings. The mother because she is full of drive and over-aggressive has little or no respect for her husband who is weak and ineffectual.

A child who finds himself in such an environment is overwhelmed by a sense of rejection. He finds himself neglected and unwanted. The father is too weak and immature to give his child effective guidance and advice. The mother is too much preoccupied with her own numerous affairs to pay any

41

attention to the child. Under such conditions he soon begins to feel alone and rejected; he is unhappy, frustrated and isolated. In time he learns that the only satisfaction he can derive is from eating, quite often from constant nibbling, and overeating. It is not too long before he begins to put on weight.

In spite of the notion that fat children are happy and carefree, this is far from the truth. Fat children are, as a rule, unhappy, insecure, maladjusted, with a strong sense of rejection and feelings of inferiority, envy and jealousy of children who are of normal weight, more graceful in figure and movement. They are always conscious of their appearance with a resultant attitude of belligerency against anyone who remarks upon their obesity.

The overweight child is emotionally tense the greater part of the time. There is a perpetually pronounced resentment against the domineering, uncaring, unappreciative mother. There is also quite often a feeling of hostility toward the mother, and for the father there is a feeling of pity and sympathy because of the mother's over-aggressive attitude toward him.

There are two principal reasons why a child will overeat. The first is as a compensation for the absence of other satisfactions. It is well known that among adults, after the loss of a loved one, after the funeral, consumption of large quantities of food helps to overcome the devastating feeling of loss and deprivation. A very interesting phenomenon has been observed in affection-starved children who have been placed in foster homes. For the first time they feel secure and accepted. They make up for years of emotional starvation by eating large quantities of food. Children who had presented problems of undereating at home are often reported by their foster parents as eating excessively. This, however, is only a temporary event until the child finds other resources, in an atmosphere of greater security.

The second reason why a child will overeat is as a means of gaining parental approval. In many instances obese children are unwanted children. The mother considers a child "good" when he takes all that she gives him. However, when he rebels against stuffing, he is "bad." Thus in the absence of genuine acceptance, the only means open to the child is to overeat to conform to his mother's conception of a good child. In this way overeating comes to mean submission to the mother's wishes.

However, this is only the beginning. The submission often leads to prolonged dependence and immaturity. The obese child is a poorly adjusted child with habits far from normal. Often he is a bed-wetter; he clings to his mother in spite of his pent-up resentment against her. He has few interests outside his eating.

A small portion of overweight children are so because of glandular or metabolic disturbances. Even in these cases diet and medication alone are not sufficient to attain good results. A child cannot be expected to readily give up his chief source of satisfaction and his only available means of struggling for his mother's approval unless he is helped to develop healthier means of gaining satisfaction. To quote Dr. Bruch again: "To be of real value, therapy should help the child grow independent and self-reliant and make constructive use of his good physical and mental endowments, so that he can find more dynamic outlets for his creative drives than the static form of physical largeness."

How can we help him to develop healthier means of gaining satisfaction? This can be done by fulfilling his need for belonging; by fulfilling his need for adequacy and by satisfying his need for worthwhileness. When these are accomplished the devastating feeling of jealousy is dissipated and the obese child is on the road to attaining adjustment.

Let us examine each of the above a little more in detail:

1. The need for belonging. All children at any age and

under whatever special disability, can increase the feeling of belonging by their own special and personal efforts at sharing. Sharing is a two-way action. It provides opportunity and encouragement for the child's personal effort to share whatever is going on around him. This attitude invites sharing with others.

2. The need for adequacy. It is important for the obese child to feel important as a doer because this helps to fulfill an important need and satisfies him emotionally so that he can break the habit of over-eating to secure satisfaction.

3. The need for a sense of worthwhileness. He must learn to do those things which give him satisfaction and he must be given opportunities to repeat them until they are established as worthwhile. He should be afforded as many of these worthwhile experiences as possible so that he can seek for himself a worthwhile way of living.

It is very important that the obese child be happy. Happiness means mental health and emotional satisfaction. This is a very important step toward abolishing the habit of over-eating. For this reason the parents should employ guidance principles which aim towards the child's happiness. They should insure some long-time goals. These goals, of course, depend upon the immaturities and maturities of the particular child. The adult should make each event in the child's day/take him a step ahead in readiness for a similar happening. He should be made more able to anticipate such a happening, more ready to accept and deal with it, and more confident and capable in understanding it. The parents should try to have the child's everyday experience expand, be it ever so little.

The long-time goals the parents should set for the child involve satisfaction in the things he undertakes. In addition there are supplementary sources of satisfaction that can be made available to the child. These are affection, respect, help and approval.

The obese child can be given a more mature outlook on life by following a few simple rules:

1. Share with him activities he initiates.

2. Give general approval as sanction and encouragement for whatever activity he may be engaging in.

3. Expressing affection for the child deepens the feeling of belonging between himself and his parents.

4. Sharing socially with the child gives this feeling of belonging in addition to the satisfaction he can get from activity and achievement.

Careful guidance on the part of the parents can prove of great help in aiding the child to find a way of life that is so emotionally satisfactory to him he will abandon the habit of overeating to gain emotional satisfaction. When his abnormal physical appearance is corrected, all unhealthy feelings connected with it will also disappear.

CHAPTER NINE

The Special Problems of the Child
with Glandular Defects

The endocrine glands exert a profound influence on the child's personality. Underactivity or overactivity of these glands, as the case may be, bring about certain well-defined changes. Thyroid deficiency results in mental retardation. The degree of mental retardation depends upon the degree of thyroid deficiency. The greater the deficiency the greater is the mental retardation.

Even in slight cases of thyroid deficiency, the changes that take place are easily recognizable. The child is very restless. Often the restlessness is so marked that he has to be restrained forcibly. He is careless with his possessions to the point of destructiveness. There is also speech disturbance such as the inability to pronounce certain letters or sounds, or speech blocking, and even complete inability to speak.

The outstanding common features in all thyroid deficient children are an extreme feeling of personal insecurity, a strong sense of responsibility, and a tendency to suffer in silence. The feeling of insecurity leads them to seek sources of protection. This accounts for the fact that some of them maintain prolonged attachment to parents, or attach themselves to other protectors.

Any threat to their security is experienced by them as an emotional shock or strain. They are quite easily upset by adverse experiences. Yet they are afraid to complain, afraid because of the disapproval this may occasion, and for this reason, they suffer in silence.

This condition can be further complicated by feelings of jealousy because they cannot adjust themselves as other children can. They feel inferior and not as capable as their playmates. Their general appearance is not at all graceful, and this further contributes to their sense of envy of others.

Fortunately, thyroid deficiency can be corrected by the administration of thyroid extract in proper doses. This corrects the gross physical defects, and, in time, also results in improved mental and emotional status of the child.

The pituitary gland also exerts a profound influence on the child's personality. As a rule, children whose pituitary glands do not function properly are cheerful, happy, and apparently contented. But their reactions are slow, and hence they may be irritating and annoying to persons who feel that their retarded response is indicative either of lack of interest or carelessness. In fact, such children, because of their slowness, may give the impression that they are mentally retarded, whereas in the majority of cases, they are really very bright. Another characteristic of these children is that they fall asleep readily; they may fall asleep in the classroom, much to the annoyance of the teacher, who attributes this symptom to indifference rather than to a lack of pituitary secretion.

The pituitary deficient child lacks aggressiveness. He is shy, gentle, easy going, timid, and artistic, traits that are usually considered effeminate, and which are in harmony with his physical appearance. He avoids strenuous physical exercise and the stress and strain of competitive work and sports. He prefers the arts and sciences.

The direct effects of pituitary deficiency on the child's personality may be intensified or altered as a result of the reaction of the child himself to his own deficiencies in growth and structure. Thus the child who, as a result of pituitary deficiency, has a submissive, passive, phlegmatic personality, may become aggressive, dominant and antisocial because of a feeling of resentment acquired as a result of the knowledge of his structural defects. Passivity, over dependence, and submissiveness may be replaced by aggressiveness, truculence, and independence, even to the point of delinquency and criminality. Such changes represent attempts to soothe the wounded ego, as well as compensation for feelings of inadequacy and inferiority. On the other hand, the feelings of inadequacy and inferiority, instead of resulting in such compensatory mechanisms, may further heighten the submissive-passive type of behavior and make the child more dependent on others and therefore less able to make normal social adjustments.

When the pituitary deficiency is marked, the administration of pituitary extracts is the best way to correct not only the physical manifestations of this deficiency but also the psychological defects that are the result of this deficiency.

The adrenal type of deficiency is distinct and set apart from the others. This type of child has coarse, thick and often curly hair. The forehead is low with a low hairline. The eyes are deeply pigmented whether they are brown, black or blue; and the pupil is unusually small. The nose of the adrenal child is well developed with large nostrils. The lips are slightly full, rich in color and warm; the teeth are large and have a tendency to decay and cavities. The tongue is thick and coarse. The head is wide across the temples, with heavy, solid jaws. The skin is dry, thick and warm. The neck is short and thick, while the chest is broad and conspicuous. The adrenal personality is possessed of almost inexhaustible amounts of energy. He never seems to tire.

The inner chemistry of the child's body is of the utmost importance in the maintenance of the proper equilibrium in mental and physical health. This is particularly true of the nervous system. It has been found that nutritional deficiency decreases mental function and nerve health. The brain requires dextrose continuously for energy, since it can oxidize no other sugar. When the brain fails to get the proper amount of this sugar, certain symptoms become manifested. These are nervousness, sleeplessness, pallor, salivation and decrease in mental activity, as well as restlessness, facial twitching, double vision, and convulsions. Psychic features are anxiety, depression, lack of concentration, thick speech, facial grimacing, emotional imbalance and hysteria.

The brain also requires a continuous supply of oxygen. When there is a decrease in the amount of oxygen, the following symptoms occur: headache, depression, apathy and drowsiness.

Thiamin deficiency also results in emotional difficulties in children. Neurasthenia is the first functional disorder seen in thiamin deficiency. It is manifested by weariness, anxiety, irritability, forgetfulness, headaches, and hypersensitivity.

Chemical and glandular factors play a very important part in the physical and psychical makeup of the child. Deficiencies and overabundance of these elements produce quite definite behavioral characteristics. When undesirable features are present, the use of the proper methods of supplying the missing and required elements may easily bring about a correction of these faults.

CHAPTER TEN

The Unique Problems of the
Left-Handed Child

The left-handed child, in addition to the problems that other children have, has quite unique problems of his own. He is a member of a minority group and as such is subjected to various pressures which in time lead to conflicts and tensions. It has been observed that often behavior disorders may result when a left-handed child is made to use his right hand. Under such conditions he cannot function with ease and naturalness. Tensions are brought about by eye strain, such as using the left eye when the right hand is forced to take over the functions of the left hand.

There is a general group of difficulties in left-handed children, who present behavior disorders. These include awkwardness, poor muscular co-ordination, irritability, restlessness, slow thinking and readily induced confusion. Among active special symptoms are slow speech, stuttering, and mirror writing. A secondary set of factors arising from these disorders are manifested in special disabilities in reading, writing, and arithmetic; and in truancy, lying and stealing.

Behavior disorders incidental to left-handedness vary according to the personal makeup of the child. The more marked difficulties arise as the direct results of maladjustment. The indirect effects of such maladjustments are, however, more significant in that they bring about increased personal social maladaptation. It has been observed, for example, that physical clumsiness may be paralleled by uncertainty with marked interference in the field of learning. This limitation in learning leads to further disturbances, including self-consciousness, a sense of inferiority and social inadequacy, with feelings of envy and jealousy. This in turn leads to further behavior disturbances.

There is ample evidence that forcing a left-handed child to use the right hand leads to definite behavior problems. For this reason, left-handed children should be allowed to remain left-handed. In some left-handed children it has been observed that when they are compelled to use the right hand there is some moderate impairment of speech, occasional slowing up, and a moderate degree of mirror writing. In some cases permanent stuttering may result from forced using of the right hand.

Left-handed children are best left alone as far as endeavoring to make them right-handed is concerned. When a child is forced to adopt the right hand under such circumstances there is a tremendous upheaval in his psychological makeup. In a short time very definite difficulties are manifested. Briefly stated they are:

1. Defects in writing, including illegibility, slowness, and writing words and sentences backwards.

2. Speech deficiencies, including slow utterance, poor enunciation, and later stuttering.

3. Reading disability with incidental slow learning.

4. Physical maladjustments, part of which are due to inherent nervous tensions and part to difficulties in adjustment. Hence there is irritability and restlessness on the one hand, and awkwardness, clumsiness and physical ineptitude on the other.

What should you do if your child is left-handed? First, never should any left-handed child be made to use the right hand. When the conversion has been made from left- to right-handedness, the child should be allowed to return to the use of his left hand. Often as a result of this approach, marked changes in behavior occur. These include a clearing up of speech difficulties in learning to read, and the removal of writing difficulties. Also there is a control of irritability and restlessness and an improvement in physical co-ordination.

Among other things observed when the left-handed child is allowed to use his left hand is that he becomes more obedient, and that stealing, lying and other antisocial behavior abate.

The earlier the return is made to the use of the left hand, the better are the results. In older children, where there has been a longer fixation of the unnatural use of the right hand, it is often more difficult to secure adjustments.

A child always functions best when he is left to exercise his natural expressions. Interference always brings about tensions and this results in behavior difficulties. It is a very good idea not to interfere in such cases.

The left-handed child is constituted in a special way as far as his brain is concerned. The mere fact that the left side and the left hand are dependent upon the natural activities of the right side of the brain, and that the right hand is dependent upon the left side of the brain suggests that there are inherent nerve tensions when these processes are reversed. When a left-handed child is forced to use his right hand, he is called upon to depend for directions on the left side of the brain, which in his case is not as well organized for this purpose as the right side of the brain.

We are then agreed that a left-handed child should be allowed to remain a left-handed child. He still has some emotional problems to face because of the fact that he is a left-handed child, a minority group in a right-handed world. He is called "lefty" or "southpaw," and he may resent these appellations. He may resent being different from other children. He may, in some cases, be jealous of children who are able to use their right hand, and whom he may consider to be more dexterous because of this ability.

A little common sense and the proper guidance can, in many cases, relieve the child of unpleasant emotional pressures. The child should be made to understand that left-handedness is not an anomaly, that a great many famous people have been left-handed, and that it is not a sign of physical or intellectual inferiority.

CHAPTER ELEVEN

The Emotional Defects of Speech Disorders

Speech is a normal human activity. If it does not develop normally or is not used correctly, it indicates that there is some underlying disturbance in the body or in the personality of the speaker. Speech disorders also result in emotional difficulties in the child. The social standard of a child is definitely determined by his speech ability and any speech impairment is a social disadvantage which may influence his entire life.

Speech develops during the first six years of life. A normal child usually begins to speak at the age of nine to twelve months, but even when speech comes later it may still be considered normal. By the age of two, a child should have started to speak.

Mutism is the first severe speech disorder. It may be the result of various conditions, the most frequent of which is deafness. A deaf child does not speak because he does not hear speech. Even a hearing impairment of more or less considerable degree may suppress the formation of speech in a child who is only hard of hearing. Most deaf-mutes have no abnormalities in their articulative organs, which would hinder the development of speech. Articulated speech can be taught them by touch and sight and many deaf-mutes learn to speak fairly well; their voices, however, retain a peculiar quality, due to lack of acoustic control. Such children may be taught to understand by lip-reading.

Children who are hard of hearing may be greatly improved

by acoustic training which increases their discrimination and understanding. This progress will also favorably influence their speech. They should also have the additional benefit of lip-reading and of hearing aids, in order to approach normal children as much as possible. As a rule, even children who are considered deaf have some hearing remnants which can be developed for better use.

Audimutism is lack of speech in children with normal hearing. It may originate from one of the following causes: 1. Subnormal intelligence; 2. injuries to the brain at birth or in early childhood; 3. malformation of the mouth and of the articulative organs; 4. extreme motor awkwardness; 5. extenuating diseases; 6. retarded general development; 7. psychic factors. In expressive audimutism the child does not speak, but understands fairly well what he hears; in receptive audimutism the child does not understand speech. Some children affected by receptive audimutism do not react to sound at all and pay no attention to speech. Others have a tendency to repeat echolike what they hear without understanding it. If the intelligence is not severely impaired, speech treatment as a rule provokes formation of sounds and words as well as understanding of speech. The therapy combines phonetic instruction with controlled play and educational guidance. In some cases it is necessary to stimulate the formation of sounds with tactile and visual help, sometimes even with artificial formation of sounds. In other cases it is sufficient to show simple pictures to the child, naming them one by one, while the child observes the therapist's mouth. Other mute children require special stimulation of the acoustic area by noises, music, speech and special acoustic training. In every case of audimutism the family background is very important and the child's life has to be adjusted to his psychological needs.

If speech develops spontaneously, but too late, this is called retarded or delayed speech development. The causes are the same as those for audimutism. Retarded speech as a rule shows several abnormal phenomena. Each period in a child's life has its own functional task; hence speech formation at a later period does not form harmoniously. At this later stage it develops more quickly, but frequently there are defects in articulation and a defective use of grammar and syntax. Speech guidance for these children is advisable till they have reached a normal level of development.

Dyslalia, which means incorrect formation of sounds, substitution of one sound for another or lack of sounds, is frequent in childhood. When the child is just learning to talk, omissions, substitutions and defects in sound formation are normal (baby talk), but this has to be overcome in due time. The use of baby talk by the family and encouraging the child to persist in it are productive of poor speech habits which may persist throughout life.

General dyslalia is a state of speech, in which most of the sounds are formed or used incorrectly. Speech may become nearly unintelligible. Defects in intelligence, defective acoustic perception, defective memory, motor awkwardness or a peculiar psychical attitude may be responsible for this and other forms of dyslalia. In order to achieve correct articulation it is often sufficient to let the child repeat simple sentences in reference to colored pictures. By observing the lips of the therapist, the child also gets visual stimulation. This simple procedure increases his attention and his understanding of speech. In other cases, it is necessary to teach correct sound formation by tactile and kinesthetic instruction. This is especially useful in children with defects in intelligence. General increase of their intelligence level will also improve their speech ability.

Especially frequent forms of dyslalia are incorrect formation of the sibilants, s, sh, z and th (lisping); these are often caused by motor awkwardness, as these sounds require specially distinct and exact articulation. They are also found in cases of impaired hearing for high tones, which are specially characteristic for the sibilants.

Children who are hard of hearing often show defects in articulation, as they do not differentiate sharply enough the sounds they hear and have not sufficient acoustic control of their own speech. Acoustic training and visual-kinesthetic teaching of correct sound formation is helpful.

Abnormal nasalization gives a disagreeable timbre to the voice, and in extreme cases may even affect the intelligibility of speech. Malformations in and around the mouth impair the ability for normal articulation, and some children affected with them show delayed speech development. They show also many defects in articulation. These are due partly to the fact that air escapes through the nose during phonation of all sounds, and partly to motor difficulties caused by abnormal development of the articulating organs. These children as a rule present a severe picture of dyslalia.

The treatment consists of showing correct sound formation, of breathing exercises and, in cases with defects of the palate, surgical correction of the condition. An excess of nasalism may be due to insufficient movements of the soft palate, either because of habit or due to paralysis. Gymnastic exercises to strengthen the velum are used in order to suppress the exaggerated nasality.

One of the most serious disorders of speech in childhood is stuttering. If stuttering persists over a long period of time, it becomes a neurotic disorder which may have far-reaching effects in later life. As a rule, there is no physical basis for stuttering. Only in rare cases does stuttering appear after an injury to the brain. Usually stuttering develops gradually on a neurotic basis.

No one is born a stutterer. Stuttering is a disability evolving with the growth of the personality. During the period of speech formation the child does not yet master his own language completely. His thoughts often form more quickly than his tongue can utter them. The words he needs to express himself come too slowly. In this embarrassing circumstance the last syllable or the last word he uses is repeated over and over until the next word is found. This is a normal occurrence in the development of speech and should be overcome in a short time. If the child does not outgrow these repetitions in due time, he may begin to observe them either spontaneously or because of the exhortations of his family, who tell him to stop. As soon as the child becomes exaggeratedly speech-conscious, he tries to suppress the repetition with an effort and with an amount of force not needed in normal speech. This symptom is called "blocking." It is always a sign that the child is conscious of something unusual in his speech. Often it is the beginning of a neurosis.

It should be emphasized that criticism of the child's speech and drawing his attention to it as well as urging him to speak are definitely harmful.

As soon as the stutterer observes his speech, the different symptoms appearing from then on are created by himself. The picture becomes more complicated; repetitions and blocking occur in different combinations; concomitant movements are made with his head and his body; he makes faces, smacks his lips and stops to look at the person he is speaking to; he flushes or becomes pale before or during speech. He may use filling words or sounds if he cannot express himself promptly. Finally, in order to avoid certain sounds or words, the stutterer may say things unrelated to his real meaning. His whole life is deeply affected. He becomes despondent, has feelings of inferiority, envy and jealousy.

In initial stages of stuttering and in very young children, it is often sufficient to slow the speech-tempo to halt its speed. Descriptions of simple pictures are useful, as they enrich the child's vocabulary. The discrepancy between expressive ability and the afflux of words is thereby removed and the child again begins to speak normally.

Vocal disorders occur in childhood most frequently in the form of hoarseness, usually as a result of the abuse of the voice through shouting and screaming. The first stage is due to exaggerated tension of the vocal organs—spastic hoarseness, which produces a harsh, noisy voice. Even vocal nodules have been observed in children before adolescence. This may give way to weakness of the vocal cords which no longer close completely and produce sounds with an overflow of breath. Breathing exercises and measures to relax vocal tension in the spastic stage are useful in restoring vocal function. In some cases the change of the voice in puberty brings the voice back to normal level.

The child suffering from speech and voice disorders also suffers from concomitant psychological disabilities. He feels peculiarly isolated in a world where other children are able to speak in a normal and accepted manner. He has feelings of inferiority, shame, and ridicule. He feels stigmatized and is extremely jealous of children who have no speech defects. Such a child requires psychological support in addition to speech training.

Speech defects may be overshadowed by other qualities which serve to give the child a feeling of emotional security. The speech-defective child can be taught to develop social graces, such as skill in playing a musical instrument, dancing, etc. He can be taught to be socially useful, to prove helpful to his playmates in those situations which require a helping hand. Teach your child to have a genuine interest in his playmates. Teach him not to make simple problems harder than they are. Everything can be solved with a sense of calmness much better than when under a sense of pressure. Teach him not to over-react to any situation which has a tendency to cause feelings of jealousy and envy. Show affection and appreciation and confidence in him, and assure him that any defect he may have does not make him less worthy and appreciated as an individual.

CHAPTER TWELVE

The Frustrating Problems of the
Hard-of-Hearing Child

Loss of hearing very often brings with it emotional problems and sometimes personality changes that are very distressing. The deafened child has new problems to meet and solve.
Unlike the blind or the grossly crippled, the hard-of-hearing
child is seldom sympathized with. More often he is ridiculed,
like the obese or the stutterer. The hard-of-hearing child, in
time, becomes suspicious, and often even paranoid. He prefers
to have people avoid him and not talk about him.

"People get mad at you when you can't hear," is a common
complaint. The most common single fear is that of being
considered stupid. At the same time, there is a great fear of
loneliness. There is an overwhelming feeling of being dis-
connected with life, of being out of tune with the rest of the
world, of living in a vacuum, so to speak.

It is strange but true that other children who can hear
normally tend to shun and ridicule the deafened child because
of his deafness and his inability to take part in childhood
games and activities. Because of this the deafened child feels
rejected and frustrated. He feels isolated through no fault
of his own, and in time he becomes quite anxious.

The hard-of-hearing child feels left out of things. The
social environment remains inexorable, forbidding and
without warmth. Difficulty in communication is a constant
source of anxiety and tension. There is a diffuse resentment

directed against the world. This could frequently be traced to a deeper dread of being resented and rejected by the world.

Anxiety in a world of sound where sound is part of everyday living, where one must hear other children in order to play with them, the inability to hear music, the radio, television, all pile tension on tension and dread on dread. Eventually this results in a sense of depressive helplessness. There is also a sense of inner horror brought on by the eternal, unyielding silence.

Lip-reading, though useful and a means of affording communication, cannot be substituted for the quickness and warmth of a world that cannot be heard. Because of this there is always partial isolation and helplessness as well as feelings of jealousy and envy of the children who can hear and take part in everyday activities and have the fun that the deafened child cannot.

One serious difficulty that the deafened child experiences is the difficulty of holding a conversation or maintaining contact with other children. The result is that it gradually becomes more difficult for him to find an outlet for his emotions. Talking with others overcomes loneliness. There is a warming sense of belonging to the world when we are able to use our senses of communication. By talking and listening to another person a sense of intimate relatedness is established. There is no doubt that through conversation isolation is lifted and attachment to outside objects can be formed.

The deafened child has considerable difficulty in expressing his problems. Talking about our inner doubts and anxieties in many cases helps to get rid of them. Ventilating our pent-up feelings through speaking of them to a sympathetic listener is a fundamental method of psychotherapy. The deafened child finds it extremely difficult to put into words his shortcomings, or his resentment against society for his frustrations—nevertheless, he does feel them very deeply. This often causes a feeling of utter frustration.

Some deafened children tend to deny their deafness and show general signs of nervousness, restlessness, sleep disturbance, hypersensitivity, irritability and impatience. How much of these symptoms can be explained by the beginning deficiency in hearing cannot easily be determined. However, we can see that for a child who is handicapped by deafness difficulties arise which can be handled in three ways: If the environment is understanding and kind, the child can face his problems and do something about them. If the environment is cold, forbidding and without sympathy, then the child tries unconsciously to build defenses against his difficulties by denying his deafness. The latter process costs a great deal of energy, and accompanies and reinforces the onset of a neurosis. A third possibility is that the family is overprotective, which is simply a sign of their own repressed hostility toward the handicapped child. This results in an inconsistent relationship with the child, at times catering to every whim, at other times not giving him a chance to have a nearly normal childhood.

Deafness present in early childhood can lead to rather severe character disorders. If the child has to repress the unpleasant thought that something is wrong with him, it is possible that character changes develop of which deceitfulness may be one. Its origin can be traced to the fact that the child deceived himself regarding his handicap. Of course, of the greatest importance is the existing unconscious hostility of the parents who cannot accept the fact that their child is not perfect. Overprotection and a sadistic meddling with anything regarding the child's life will be understood by the child's unconscious. The result may be either a passive feminine attitude with considerable resentment and neurotic traits and symptoms, or, on the other hand, psychopathic character traits and paranoid aggressive tendencies.

Deafness brings a certain amount of physical insecurity

but it is interesting that deaf children on the whole seem less prone to fears than normal children. This may be because there is less possibility of spreading tales of imaginary dangers, of witches and bogey men and fewer accounts of accidents and fires.

Because the deafened children are relatively few in number they are in the position of a minority group and as such are subjected to all the pressures of a minority group. With this there are feelings of not-belonging, of being discriminated against, of not enjoying all the privileges of the majority. This further fosters feelings of jealousy and envy of those who are able to enjoy the advantages of the majority.

Healthy adaptation to hearing loss involves an integrated habitual striving to overcome the limitations imposed by the loss of hearing. Some children overcompensate by an effort to batter down the barriers to the outside world by being jolly, vociferous, speaking rather than trying to listen. Quite a few children deny their hearing loss and try by various evasions to make this less apparent. A retreat from society is another method used by some children to compensate for their loss of hearing. All these skirt the problem. They do not solve the real difficulties of the deafened child.

What can be done to make the life of the deafened child more bearable? The parents can point out three assets as a compensation for deafness:

1. Deafness decreases distraction and increases concentration. Thereby one is able to do better work. Creative work in the arts and sciences is also encouraged by decrease in hearing acuity. Distraction being eliminated, persistence is encouraged in working habits and much better results are thus possible.

2. Deafness fosters constructive thought. Meditation is encouraged. Creative thinking can more readily be applied to living a better and happier life.

3. The interpretive capacity of the other senses may be increased. Sight, taste, touch and smell can be used to increased advantage in the adventure of living.

Fortunately, modern science has developed more effective methods of treating the deaf. The fenestration operation is of considerable value in many cases of deafness. Medication with hormones, vitamins and other products are of value in other types of deafness. Hearing aids have also been improved to a considerable degree. Speech-reading is the last resort, but it does establish a means of communication and lessens the sense of helpless isolation. An inner sense of determination to overcome the shortcomings of being deaf is also of value. This together with the various methods that science affords today in overcoming deafness to a greater or lesser extent can, in time, abolish almost all of the symptoms of emotional tension, anxiety, jealousy and frustration.

CHAPTER THIRTEEN

The Pressing Problems of the Child
with Nerve Disorders

Nerve disorders of various kinds are not too uncommon in childhood. In this chapter we shall consider epilepsy, cerebral palsy and chorea as examples of typical nerve disorders in children and the emotional problems they create.

Epilepsy is an ailment which is one of the rather serious disabilities of childhood. It is characterized by a periodic occurrence of temporary loss of consciousness with or without fits or convulsions. Epileptic attacks may be divided roughly into three groups. Some children may have only one type of seizure but it is rather common for the afflicted child to suffer with two or three types of spells. The three types of attack are 1. petit mal, 2. grand mal and 3. psychic equivalent or psychomotor attacks.

Petit mal attacks, which are characteristically a disease of childhood, are accompanied by transient clouding of consciousness lasting only a few seconds, with or without movements of the head, eyes and arms and legs. A grand mal attack is quite varied. Characteristically these attacks are ushered in by a warning (aura) and are followed by a sudden loss of consciousness, with convulsive movements of the entire body. Psychic equivalent, or psychomotor attacks, is a form of epilepsy which has none of the characteristics of the previous two types. The milder psychomotor attacks are often confused with petit mal but they differ from the latter in that the duration of the period of mental confusion is greater and the muscular movements are more widespread. They differ from the grand mal attacks in that the child does not fall to the ground in a fit with complete loss of consciousness. In the severer forms of psychic equivalents, the child may be in a clouded state for many hours and perform acts of which he is entirely unaware.

Epilepsy is an ailment which usually is of several years duration. The period of treatment in the majority of children is measured in terms of years or sometimes of a life time. Quite a few children become discouraged because of this disease; they have feelings of inferiority, shame and unworthiness because they feel set apart from normal children. The outstanding feeling is one of jealousy of normal children who are able to enjoy all the activities of childhood without the constant dread of having a "fit." Children should be encouraged to use all their resources to overcome their feelings of inferiority and self-consciousness.

The emotional life of the epileptic child is different from that of the normal child. Usually some emotional instability is apparent, and a rather immature intellectual approach to problems is customarily employed. There is evidence that the inner life is less rich, and that less inner stability exists. Interest in social contacts is evident, but an egocentric, impulsive approach characterizes the response, less than the desired amount of social adaptability and conformity being apparent.

The epileptic child should be kept in school unless the frequency of attacks unduly disturbs the routine of the class room, or unless mental deterioration requires special treatment. Education of other members of the family in regard to their attitude toward the child's illness is of great importance. Excessive attention and oversolicitude should be eliminated and the family should not be allowed to make a chronic invalid of the child.

Cerebral palsy is another nerve disorder which brings with it special childhood problems. Cerebral palsy is a rather crippling disease with quite severe emotional disturbances. The child with cerebral palsy must be treated and trained for many years to overcome his rather severe disabilities.

The program for the cerebral palsy child has as its objective the restoration of the child to his maximum physical, mental, emotional and social capabilities. The four basic physical requirements for daily living are the ability to walk, self-care, the maximum use of the hands, and adequate speech. The child with cerebral palsy feels extremely helpless and useless with these severe handicaps and is extremely envious and jealous of his brothers and sisters who are able to walk, talk and use their bodies with ease. He attains a feeling of inferiority and isolation. He feels left out of things and out of life.

The parents of the cerebral palsy child can do a great deal to help him emotionally. Confidently expecting the child to succeed strengthens his effort to succeed, even when he is severely handicapped. General approval, by giving sanction, assurance, or appreciation, encourages the child to try to overcome the limits of his physical capacities. Preparing in advance for the child's success in a physical action enables him to get the best results from any effort he may put forth. Sometimes giving more help than is needed to complete an undertaking makes it pleasant and satisfying to the handicapped child. The child handicapped with cerebral palsy can be made to realize that he can lead a fairly normal life within his physical capabilities. This will help to establish him on a more rational emotional basis.

Chorea is another not too uncommon nerve disorder in childhood. Many children suffering with chorea are also emotionally disturbed. They are overactive, restless, aggressive. They are emotionally unstable, tire easily, have a short attention span and poor concentration. These children, because of their nerve disorder, acquire a sense of being different, of not belonging, with subsequent feelings of inferiority and active jealousy of other children who are free of their convulsive, jerky movements.

Such children are constantly thwarted by their own poor performance and hounded by the reactions of impatient and intolerant parents. As a result they turn to other compensations, usually undesirable behavior and mischief, or they may withdraw into themselves. Continued lack of success embitters them. Their emotional irritability and excitability can create even more misery for them, depending upon the responses aroused in others. Frequently they are beaten, deprived, ostracized for traits and behavior beyond their own power to mend. Continual rebuffs and hostility to an organically irritable, uncontrolled and destructive child only serve to aggravate his emotional upheaval.

What can be done to help the emotionally disturbed child suffering from chorea? The parents should not attempt to coerce or change the child. They should adjust the requirements placed upon him to his capacity of performance. When the impossible is no longer expected of him, the tensions lessen all around.

In general, there are several basic principles which operate effectively in the guidance of children handicapped with nerve disorders:

1. Adult affection for a child builds a feeling of security. The child feels sure that to that adult he is important as a person, no matter how handicapped he may be. He belongs to that adult and that adult belongs to him, and this sense of belonging frees him to be himself.

2. Adult respect for a child builds a feeling of adequacy. He feels an adult's confident expectation that he can and

will do well in his undertakings. He therefore expects to succeed and will put forth his best effort. With each such success he places more confidence in his parents' expecting only what he can deliver and in his own confidence to do as the adult expects. Adult respect both for his limitations and his capacities builds self-confidence and self-respect. A child who discovers new and worthwhile activities through adult interest and help expects to find satisfaction in affairs that these adults encourage and approve.

CHAPTER FOURTEEN

The Special Problems of
the Maladjusted Child

Children, just like adults, may deviate from normal behavior. They may indulge in actions which are not socially useful or socially acceptable. Quite often they will not act for the best interests of the group in which they move. This type of disturbing behavior of the child is directed toward one of four possible goals. The maladjusted child acts in the way he does to: 1. gain attention, 2. demonstrate his power or superiority, 3. punish or get even and 4. give up in complete discouragement.

The great majority of children use some methods of getting attention. They do this because they feel they have to. Young children cannot attract attention to themselves by doing something socially useful. The only way a young child can feel accepted and a part of his family is by means of the older members of the family. Most children feel that they must have constant proof of their acceptance. This a child gains by demonstrations of affection or by directing attention toward himself. However, none of these methods usually increase his feelings of strength, self-reliance and self-confidence. He still feels somehow that he requires constant new proof that he is still being accepted. At first he will always try socially accepted means of gaining this attention. When those fail he will begin to employ methods that are not regarded as socially acceptable.

Even if these methods of gaining attention bring punishment, the neglected child will gladly accept this punishment. Most children prefer to be beaten rather than ignored. Even being beaten means that some sort of attention is being paid to the child. To be ignored and treated indifferently is the worst thing that can happen to a child.

After having tried legitimate and socially acceptable methods of gaining attention and having failed, the child will embark upon a course of action that is disturbing and annoying. For a while the parents may tolerate these actions without provocation. However, if these actions persist, the parents lose patience and punish him. At this time the child changes his goal, and the child and the parents become deadlocked in a struggle for power and superiority. The child tries to convince his parents that he can do what he wants, and they will not be able to stop him. Or he may seek to demonstrate that his parents cannot bend him to their will. If he succeeds in this way, he has won his point; he has gained attention and his goal. If he does not succeed, he will use other and stronger methods to attain his goal. His maladjustment becomes more obvious, his actions are more hostile, and the emotions involved are more violent.

If neither side gives in in this struggle between child and parents, the struggle grows more intense. The parents use all sorts of methods to punish and subjugate the child. This mutual hatred and antagonism becomes rather intense. It may become so strong that no pleasant experience is left to maintain a feeling of belonging, of friendliness or cooperation. When this has occurred, the child becomes vengeful. He wants to hurt others, to get even. He no longer hopes to gain attention. He feels ostracized and disliked and finds his only gratification in hurting others. If he cannot make them love him, he can make them hate him. Children of this type are the most violent and vicious. They know where it hurts most and they take advantage of the vulnerability of their opponents. Power and force impress them no longer. They are defiant and destructive. As they are sure from the beginning that nobody likes them, they provoke anyone with whom they come in contact to reject them. They regard it as a triumph when they are considered nasty. That is the only triumph they can obtain, the only one they seek.

The child who is inclined to be passive will not engage in open warfare. If his antagonism is successfully beaten down, he may be discouraged to such an extent that he cannot hope for any recognition whatsoever. He gives up entirely. As the hostility is not openly shown, he may provoke less antagonism. However, this lack of acute disturbance does not mean that his maladjustment is less grave than the child who is openly hostile. Both are indulging in socially unacceptable actions.

According to Dr. Rudolf Dreikurs, maladjusted children may be classified as active and passive, and they may use constructive or destructive methods. The choice of constructive or destructive methods depends on the child's feeling of being accepted or rejected by others; his antagonism is always expressed in destructive acts. In the main, it is this feeling of acceptance or rejection which is the active factor in swinging from constructive to destructive methods. On the other hand, active or passive behavior indicates the amount of courage. Passivity is always based on personal discouragement. Thus, according to Dr. Dreikurs, the combination of the two pairs of factors leads to four types of behavior patterns:

1. Active-constructive.
2. Active-destructive.
3. Passive-constructive.
4. Passive-destructive.

The above sequence is based on the actual progression of maladjustment. The tendency is to regard an active-destructive child as much worse than a passive-constructive one.

This is not always true. If the child's antisocial attitude has not developed too far, as in cases of attention-getting, he can be induced with relative ease to change his destructive methods into constructive ones. However, it is very difficult to change a passive child into an active one. The passive-constructive child is less of a nuisance. However he certainly needs more assistance in developing courage and self-confidence.

The active-constructive child is more appreciated by all with whom he comes in contact. Actually he is not as good as he seems to be. He is trying very hard to make an impression of excellence in order to gain praise and appreciation. Should he fail to get it, his shortcomings are immediately noticeable. He starts to misbehave. He is not content merely to be equal. He feels that he must excel; if he does not, he feels lost. His desire for perfection, for propriety and superiority is often fostered by parents who encourage such traits.

There is no doubt that this group of over-ambitious children develops active-destructive methods when their efforts to attract attention with methods that are socially acceptable fail. They often try the most unusual ways to push themselves forward when they are encouraged in the field of useful achievement. They become show-offs and clowns. They use all the methods they can think of to attract attention to themselves. Their behavior is a mechanism of attracting attention, and when this goal is attained, they become normal behaving children again.

Another rather important group consists of the children who use passive-constructive methods to gain attention. So subtle are their actions that many parents and teachers do not recognize these children as misbehaving. They are very pleasant, full of charm and quite submissive. These traits are found more in girls than in boys, and when boys have them, they are considered as effeminate. In spite of the fact that this type of child is not as unpleasant as the active-destructive one, he nevertheless requires more efforts for adjustment.

A child who seeks attention with passive-destructive methods is generally so much discouraged and feels so rejected—mostly through the methods which are used with him—that he becomes completely frustrated and discouraged. His bashfulness, instability, lack of concentration and ability, self-indulgence and frivolity, his fearfulness, his eating difficulties, and his backwardness in taking care of himself and in developing skills, make him the most difficult child in this group.

The child does not know why he behaves in a certain way. It is useless to ask a child, "Why did you do it?" When he answers, "I do not know," it is generally true. The child follows his impulses without a clear realization of his motives. If he tries to give an explanation for his behavior, his explanations are mostly rationalizations and excuses, but not the real reasons. Instead of asking the child why he did something, one must explain it to him. The child should be made aware not of the cause but of the purpose of his behavior. Reasons such as being jealous, lacking self-confidence, feeling rejected or feeling guilty are of little meaning to the child. His reaction is entirely different when his purposes and goals are disclosed to him. He may not acknowledge that this is so verbally, but his expression gives him away. Disclosure of this kind leads to an immediate change in the particular behavior, especially in a young child.

The child must be approached in a friendly way without belittling him. The disclosure should never impress the child as fault-finding. It is advisable not to make a definite statement, but to start the remark as a vague conjecture. "I wonder if you are not a little jealous," or "I wonder if you don't want to get attention, to show that you're the big boss."

When the child's goal in his misbehavior is recognized, treatment is begun. Children who drive for attention must learn to become independent by recognizing that contributing and not receiving is the most effective way to attain social status. An attempt should be made to help children become active and to change destructive methods into constructive ones until the child is able to overcome the need for any special attention.

Children who drive for power should no longer be exposed to power and pressure, against which they have successfully rebelled and still rebel. Acknowledging their value and even their power makes them self-confident so that they no longer require verification of their power.

Children who want to punish and get even are usually convinced that nobody likes them or will ever like them. They are extremely jealous and frustrated. Helping them involves a long process of demonstrating that they are and can be liked. Children who give up in discouragement have to be brought back slowly to the realization of their abilities and potentialities.

CHAPTER FIFTEEN

Jealousy and Sibling Rivalry

Jealousy among siblings is natural. It is more common in the first-born than in later born children since first-born children, during the period when they are only children, become accustomed to the undivided attention of their parents. It is more frequent in small than in large families where the children quickly learn to share the parental interest. The age difference between siblings is of considerable importance. Jealousy is more likely to be severe when the age difference between the children is from one and one-half to three years than when this is greater or less although there are many exceptions. When the older child is less than 18 months at the time of birth of a younger sibling, he has not, in most instances, become fully aware of the parental attention and affection. When the age difference is greater than three years the older child ordinarily feels secure in his parents' affection and is beginning to lose some of his dependence on his parents.

Jealousy is apt to be more severe among siblings of the same sex than in brother-sister combinations where there is less likely to be a clash of interests. It is seen where parents show favoritism or animosity toward a child and where they make invidious comparisons between the children.

The severity of the rivalry reaction depends, to a large extent, on the degree to which the child is dependent on the mother. Hence, jealousy is especially well-marked in the over-protected child. It is, however, seen whenever the child has been badly brought up and, in such cases, it serves as one of many outlets for the child's emotional discomfort.

The behavior of the jealous older child is characterized 1. by hostility toward the younger child, 2. by a desire to relive the pleasures and advantages enjoyed by the younger child, and 3. by excessive demands for parental attention. Hostility may be overt and manifest itself by attacks on the younger child, or it may be concealed. The child, made to realize the undesirability of his hostility, may develop guilt feelings. Excessive fearfulness sometimes results from the child's appreciation of his own hostile impulses toward a sibling.

Of considerable interest are the infantile responses frequently seen in older children following the birth of a sibling. The older child will often wet and soil himself, though previously fully trained, and he frequently chooses the parental lap for this purpose. There are demands to be diapered, to be fed, etc.

Since sibling rivalry is rarely troublesome in a well brought-up child, it is apparent that the most important factor in prevention is proper child rearing. Parents should be taught the simple principles on which child development is based. They should be instructed in the needs of the child to develop at his own rate and they should understand the harmful effects of trying to accelerate or retard developmental tempo. They should become aware that the child has needs, mental, motor and emotional, which must be gratified. They should know that the child requires guidance and discipline. Efforts should be made to relieve parental tension and anxiety about the child and a natural affectionate attitude should be encouraged.

Certain preparatory suggestions before the arrival of another infant may be helpful. The older child should be informed of the expected arrival of the newcomer and should know that the mother is to go to the hospital for this purpose.

Emphasis should be placed on his own maturity and on the helplessness of the baby. If he is to be moved out of his room or his crib to make way for the new baby, the change should be made several weeks before the expected birth.

Many parents fail to understand that jealousy toward a new sibling is natural. In their well-intentioned desire to build for family unity, they worry and exert themselves unduly about a situation which is unimportant and which will right itself in time. In such instances an explanation of the mechanics involved and assurances of its normality are ordinarily sufficient in allaying parental agitation.

Following the birth of a new sibling the older child needs reassurance of parental affection and he requires attention and privileges on a level corresponding to his developmental status. The parents should see to it that he receives a due share of their interest and that he is not forgotten in the excitement incident to the arrival of a new baby.

Where jealousy is intense it may be advisable for the mother to avoid nursing or otherwise ministering to the baby in the older child's presence; but he should not feel that he is being excluded. The father can help greatly by assuming a more active role in the child's life, thereby giving the child additional affection and attention on a more mature level.

CHAPTER SIXTEEN

The Unwanted Child

The unwanted child is unwanted for one or more of several reasons. In general, unwanted children may be any of the following:

1. No child wanted—in other words, one or both parents may not wish any child or may not want a child at this particular time.

2. Parents wish a boy, and a girl is born; consequently the girl is unwanted.

3. Parents wish a girl and a boy is born, hence the boy is unwanted.

The unwanted child starts life under a disadvantage, a disadvantage that may sometimes lead to the most serious consequences both to himself and to society. The unwanted or rejected child is destined on the average to show strong aggressive traits, to be hostile and antagonistic towards those with whom he must have dealings, to be envious and jealous of children who are wanted and loved, to develop tendencies which may lead to delinquency. Over-submissive behavior and neuroses are also reaction patterns of the unwanted child.

Getting back to the question of rejection as evidenced by unwilling mothers or unwilling fathers, it may be shown openly despite the disapproval of society. It is frequently encountered when the baby is not planned for, but it is also seen at other times. It is evidenced by the fact that the young mother turns away from her newly born infant and refuses to nurse it, neglects to keep it clean or to train it adequately in basic habits. She punishes it severely and refuses to play with it. She lets her time be taken up by matters outside the home. She is indifferent to the child's illnesses; she hates to touch or caress it. She is not interested in its education. She may become jealous of the child if it is a girl, and nag it if it is a son.

In many instances the birth of an unwanted or unwelcomed child is proclaimed as such. Sometimes the father rejects the child when it seems to have occasioned the death of the mother, and this persists for many years.

Quite often the unwanted child is unwanted primarily because of the mother's unhappy adjustment to marriage. This in turn is usually a result of immaturity and emotional instability on the part of one or both parents. The mother's handling is most frequently inconsistent, wavering between over-protective and hostile behavior. The children, in turn, exhibit a mixture of aggressive, antisocial, as well as submissive, neurotic symptoms. In addition, it is found that aggressive behavior occurs more frequently when the parental handling is consistently hostile, while submissive behavior occurs more frequently when the parental handling is consistently protective.

A less obvious form of rejection is disguised and appears as over-protection. This may allow the mother to express her hatreds against the child and at the same time compensate as a penance so as to appease her guilt feelings. Such a mother broods constantly over a child, cannot bear to have it out of her sight, and lives forever in the fear that some evil will befall it. Even though she may be an intelligent woman, she may fear that the child is not bright mentally when there is no evidence to this effect.

There are several predisposing factors in a woman who rejects her child: 1. Childhood experiences in which she herself was rejected by her own parents. 2. Childhood experiences which gave rise to marked jealousy, rivalry, antagonism between herself and siblings. 3. Marked incompatibility on one score or another between herself and her husband—the father of her children. The third and last factor noted is almost a universal one, but one is not to infer, therefore, that it is a universal cause. There are far too many instances when, in spite of marital difficulties, there is no element of rejection. One can include marital disharmony as more often contributory than causative, and in all probability one or both of the other two factors must as a rule be operative if the rejection mechanism is to become significantly manifest.

Let us consider the mechanism of rejection in greater detail. Rejection can be defined in terms of both feeling and behavior. In terms of feeling, rejection refers to the hate and hostility which a parent feels toward a child. In terms of behavior, a parent rejects a child when he or she is aggressive and hostile toward it and fails to give it adequate care and protection. More specifically, a parent rejects a child by neglecting it, by separating himself from the child, by denying the child's wishes, by punishment, by maltreatment, or by threats of these, by humiliating the child and by more general expressions and a rejecting attitude.

Rejection refers to considerably more than the mere fact that a child may not be wanted at birth. It is the general term referring to all negative or harmful attitudes that a parent might adopt towards a child. Parents show their negative attitude by neglecting the child, failing to provide adequate food, clothing or training, or failing to supervise the child's development.

A form of rejection with serious consequences is found in the mother's separating herself from the child as in deserting the child or placing it in some foster home, institute, boarding school, or leaving the child to the care of others. Rejection may also be shown in denying the child gratification, as through discontinuance of breast feeding, withholding gifts, or denying the child pleasure.

Punishment of the child and maltreating him, whether physical or mental, is another evidence of rejection. Frequently threats of separation or punishment have a great or even greater effect on the child than the act itself. Humiliation of the child through criticism, ridicule, blaming, comparing the child unfavorably with siblings, or meeting the child's advances with coolness or rebuffs, are all forms of rejection. A parent may show her feelings towards a child by showing annoyance with the child, criticizing it to others, being suspicious of the child's behavior, and in general failing to find satisfaction or pleasure in it.

Rejection is fundamentally the feeling that the parent has for the child which may express itself in various forms of behavior. In some instances the rejection is so pronounced that expressions of it can easily be observed. Usually, however, parents feel somewhat guilty about harboring hostile feelings toward a child, and are careful not to exhibit rejection openly. Sometimes tendencies toward rejection are disguised by rationalization, as when a parent explains that the child is being sent away to school for its own good.

Rejection should not be thought of as a fixed and permanent attitude of a parent toward a child. It is one that may persist over a long period of time, but on the other hand, it may wax and wane. Some parents reject a child at birth only to find that the care of the infant arouses unsuspected feelings of love. Sometimes parents first reject a child at the age of two or three, when it begins to assert itself, or later when the child meets the challenge of school. Some parents have a tendency to reject a child when it approaches adolescence, and the maturity of the child becomes a threat to the parents' own needs.

To the child, rejection is a frustration, and he responds to it as he responds to any frustrating circumstance. A common response to rejection is show-off behavior, which is calculated in the first place to win the parents' love, and if this fails, at least to have the parents' attention which is the nearest token of love that he can win. Show-off behavior in the school or on the playground may be a displaced attempt to win a place in someone's affection, and it is an indication that the child fundamentally is rejected. As is the case with any frustration, rejection results in aggressiveness. The aggressive child likewise is attempting to win by force the emotional security that is so necessary for his peace of mind. The rejected child is also plagued by feelings of jealousy of children who are wanted and appreciated. Rejection also leads to unstable and psychopathic tendencies. Rejected children may frequently be picked out in the classroom as those who are restless and find it necessary to move about the room. Hyperactive children frequently are rejected.

On the other hand, as is well known, many children raise defenses against their own aggressive tendencies and adopt the reaction formation of extreme submissiveness, politeness and docility.

Factors which are responsible for a parent's rejecting a child may be divided into the immediate and the personality factor. Of the immediate factors, a child may be neglected because it is an economic burden to the parents, because the parents' work requires their absence from the home for part of the day, because of the mother's ill health, or because the child interferes with the activities and aspirations of the parents.

A more fundamental explanation for rejection may be found in the personality of the parents. In many cases parents adopt their hostile attitudes toward their children as a displacement of similar negative attitudes, usually of an unconscious nature, which they had at an early age toward their siblings. Not infrequently marriage causes a repetition of the earlier triangular situation, and it is found that the parents are displaying to their children the hatred which they held at an earlier age toward a member of their own family. Sometimes parents project the hatred which they are unwilling to recognize in themselves onto their children.

To overcome the adverse effects of rejection the parents have recourse to simply reversing their attitude and expressing one of acceptance. Acceptance refers to the positive and constructive attitude, feelings, and behavior of a parent toward a child, and has considerable significance in helping the child achieve a measure of emotional security and develop its traits of personality. Parental acceptance refers fundamentally to the feeling that a parent has for the child, which will show itself in parental attitudes and behavior.

Following are some of the usual ways in which parental acceptance is expressed. Parents who accept their children find pleasure in them and express that pleasure in word and deed. They praise their child to others. They enjoy doing things with the child, and take interest in his growth and development, and in his pleasures and achievements. The accepting parent provides adequate care and protection for his child; he is generous. The accepting mother is generous with her milk following birth, and takes pleasure in sharing experiences and benefits with the child. The accepting parent shows his fondness for the child by tokens of affection through physical contact—he expresses fondness through stroking and petting. The accepting parent is encouraging and shows appreciation for every step in growth and achievement that the child takes.

The accepted child in general tends to show a number of admirable characteristics. He tends to be socialized, and, in turn, makes himself acceptable to others. He tends to be co-operative in social undertakings. The accepted child tends to develop good moral character, and is honest, dependable, and truthful. The accepted child tends to be stable, is calm and deliberate in bearing, and is not readily excited or confused when under stress. The accepted child evinces enthusiasm in any activity in which he is engaged. In general, he is careful of the property and comfort of others. He tends to feel in harmony with these behavioral trends. He is secure and self-confident, and does not indulge in self pity. He tends to be cheerful and optimistic. He is free of jealousy and envy. He evaluates himself realistically—neither over-estimating nor underestimating himself in relation to others. The accepted child tends on the whole to be contented and happy.

Accepting parents tend on the whole to be well adjusted. Their marital relationships tend to be harmonious and satisfying, and they bring from their childhood personalities which are normal rather than neurotic. The parents who accept their children treat their children objectively, and are not forced to use their children as a way of working off some of their own unmet needs.

CHAPTER SEVENTEEN

The Child Whose Parents
Are Divorced

The child whose parents are divorced has unique emotional problems to cope with. He is the victim of two adults who had problems and difficulties which they felt could be solved only in divorce; his home life has been disrupted. Children from divorced homes are more apt to be subjected to unhealthy social conditions than children whose homes are intact.

On the whole, it has been found that children from divorced homes contribute more than their quota to the ranks of delinquents, while they appear less frequently in groups of superior young people. It has been ascertained that children of divorced (or even of unhappily married) parents are more likely to make failures in their own marriages.

If the children of divorced parents are so likely to display unfavorable traits of personality and character, so likely to become delinquent, so likely to fail in important social adjustments, the question arises as to why this is so. There are a great many contributory factors. Some of these are: educational and economic difficulties brought about by the divorce, lack of parental control and supervision, divided loyalty (children being made the battleground of parents), difficulty of establishing new loyalties (the step-parent problem), destruction of ideals, lack of emotional security, etc.

Another factor is the personality make-up of the parents

of the child. Divorcees consist of all kinds of people but on the average fall below the happily married part of the population in conspicuous ways. Parents who are ready to seek a divorce are, in quite a few instances, suffering from some sort of emotional instability. When this is the case, the children are likely to become infected with some sort of emotional instability.

All children learn by example, precept and association. The environment in which the child finds himself has a great deal to do with shaping his personality and character. No human being is born into the world with a moral sense or a knowledge of morals or moral concepts. Whatever moral sense we have is the result of inculcation. Morals may be taught directly or indirectly. Our responsibility to ourselves as individuals and to those among whom we live, and the corresponding responsibility of others toward us, defines in a broad sense what we mean by morals.

What we accept as morals, is what we are taught morals are, by precept, by example, by family reactions. The child who accepts the ethical formula handed down to him and who adjusts to the norms of the people among whom he lives and the family in which he is being raised, is deemed to be living a normal life. His moral and emotional outlook is greatly influenced by those of his parents.

No child is born into the world conditioned. Conditioning is the result of processes applied by adults in the development of the child's personality. Actually there is no application of any specific process. The child imbibes all that surrounds him. If conditions are wholesome and good, he may develop into a human being conditioned to live a good life. If, however, home conditions are unsatisfactory, such as those brought about by a home broken up because of divorce, he may develop a personality that will prevent his adjustment to normal life, and in more extreme cases may engage in antisocial conduct, aggression and delinquency. The child in a home broken up because of divorce feels different from those children whose parents are living together. He feels outcast, a pariah, inferior, and intensely jealous of children whose parents are able to give them the affection and guidance they require.

The child who comes from a home disrupted by divorce is quite often a neglected child. Among the causes contributing to juvenile misconduct is neglect. The neglect which will affect the conduct of a child is not limited to a failure to provide the physical necessities that build strong bodies. To neglect a child's emotional growth, to fail in stimulating a sense of personal and communal responsibility, is apt to affect the conduct of a child more disastrously than physical neglect.

Family morale is always an important factor in the emotional and spiritual growth of the child. Family morale cannot exist in a home disrupted by divorce. It is in the small group such as the family that the matter of individual morale and the variability from individual to individual becomes particularly important. Individual differences naturally exist in any group. Some fluctuations in individual morale from time to time also occur as circumstances and interpersonal relationships change, or as the objectives and activities of the group shift from one emphasis to another. We are particularly concerned with these individual differences and fluctuations in individual morale with respect to the common purposes and activities of the family group.

A child with high family morale is one who is happily adjusted in his home life. His relationships with the other family members and particularly with his parents from his point of view are characterized by mutual confidence, affection and congeniality. His desires, purposes and ambitions are to a relatively high degree integrated with, and not arrayed against, those of the family group.

The personality adjustments of the parents undoubtedly

are among the most important single factors determining the level of family morale. Personality adjustments of divorced parents are nil, and consequently the family morale is non-existent.

It is extremely important from the standpoint of child welfare and family success, that parents pay special attention to family morale. They must, first of all, realize that for each child in the family the problem is unique. The general adjustment situation—the family role which he must assume and the difficulties and satisfactions involved—as well as his original temperament and his natural endowment, all combine to make his case different from every other. It is through insight into the unique problem of each individual child that the parent is able to establish helpful relationships with all his children and insure a happy and harmonious family life. This is not possible when the parents are divorced.

In the closely knit family, the goals and activities of the family are accepted as worthy and important by the family members. Individual purposes are usually integrated with those of the group, and the leadership of the parents is accepted with confidence. In short, family morale is high. In such a family situation numerous experiences in co-operative activity and other forms of social interaction are provided for the children. Thus, high family morale is essential to what is perhaps the most important remaining function of the family, namely, to foster desirable personality adjustment and social development. This certainly is an utter impossibility in cases where the child is a victim of divorce.

The child of divorced parents is very often an insecure child; he feels insecure because of the extremely unstable home situation. This feeling of insecurity is further fostered by the circumstance where the child is shifted from place to place or from one home to another because of the divorced parents.

The child needs to feel secure in order to develop properly.

The home and the family circle should provide the first and final basis of security for him. He should feel that home is a place where he can go and be welcome and protected. This is possible only when the parents are living together and can give the child the affection, protection and guidance he needs. When this is not the case, the child will, in quite a few instances, react with feelings of insecurity, inferiority, emotional instability and jealousy. The child of divorced parents is very often a jealous child, jealous of the loss of home conditions that are essential for his proper development, and of other children who have them.

CHAPTER EIGHTEEN

The Adopted Child

Legal adoption of children is largely a matter of recent history, and it is quite a common practice in our culture. The child who is adopted has certain emotional problems that other children do not have. The mere fact that he is an adopted child makes him feel that he has lacking in him certain qualities that other children possess.

It has always been considered desirable to tell an adopted child, upon his reaching an age of understanding, that he is adopted. The reaction to the knowledge that he is adopted is always quite an emotional one. Upon being acquainted with the fact, the child may demonstrate a period of doubt concerning his parentage, or a persistence of the doubt even after the problem has been consciously faced. In some cases, there may be marked difficulty of adjustment to other parent substitutes and subsequent foster homes.

The adopted child at one time or another has conscious fantasies concerning his original parents. This may be in the nature of the mother coming to claim the son, or of communication with the parent, or of speculative fantasies concerning the possible appearance of the parents. There may be fantasies of finding the mother, and atonement and forgiveness. Or there may be fantasies of the parents not wanting the child. However, there is very seldom any conscious fantasy of revenge for having been deserted.

How does a child react when first learning that he is

adopted? There are many and varied reactions. Sometimes there is resentment against the foster parents, and sometimes the adopted child may run away from home. The home desertion may be motivated by conscious resentment, or may be purposeless and apparently irrational. In some cases a strong hostility has been repressed and then re-directed in an antisocial manner.

It is no doubt true that many normal children developing in normal families often have transient fantasies of doubt concerning their parentage. This is probably due to transient hostilities or feelings of rejection which may be generated even in the course of the most smoothly functioning family unit. Under ordinary circumstances, however, the fundamental security and love relationships in a normal home will always suffice to dissipate these fantasies.

It is quite possible that neighbors and relatives can accidentally drop hints to an adopted child which might set a train of doubting fantasy going; or that the foster parents, in spite of strong love for a foster child, may still be unable to prevent an alert child from feeling a certain lack of fundamental security in the relationship. Quite a few adopted children demonstrate this doubt.

The confirmation of the doubt is of course the major trauma. The emotional security within the family unit is badly shaken, and the attitudes to authority and society suffer. Perhaps the most pernicious result is the development of an ambivalent attitude to the foster parents, love for past care and affection, and hate for the withdrawal of the security of that relationship. This resentment and hostility may be expressed by acts against the foster parents or against society.

In general, an adopted child on first learning that he is adopted will react in the following manner:

1. A preliminary period of uncertainty of parentage.

2. Resentment at not having been previously informed of a fact of tremendous importance.

3. Fantasies of the real parents coming to claim him.

4. Onset of disturbed behavior and emotional upset after the disclosure.

5. A desire to run away from home, sometimes carried out.

6. Fantasies of the foster parents not wanting him, a belief very often not justified by the foster parents' real attitude.

The adopted child is very often a jealous child, jealous of other children who have their real parents taking care of them. He quite often feels unwanted and rejected because of the fact that his real parents deserted him. Sometimes he feels inferior and he is very sensitive of the fact that he is an adopted child.

How is one to help the adopted child over his emotional upsets on learning that he is adopted? He can be made to realize that an adopted child is a special kind of child. Fathers and mothers have to take what they can get when they have their own children. They have no choice. But an adopted child is chosen by his parents because he needed them, and they love him the more for it.

The adopted child feels unimportant because of the subconscious feeling of having been rejected and deserted by his real parents. The prime objective, then, is to inculcate in the adopted child a sense of importance. The greater the child's feeling of importance, the more he will feel that he is accepted, the greater will be the sociality of his striving and the greater the satisfaction he will derive from it.

When the child is encouraged in his striving for importance, he is also called upon to develop his given potentialities. This will give him an urge to grow, to increase his usefulness and dignity as an individual. All children have the capacity as well as the will to develop their potentialities, and when impetus is given to this will to develop their inner resources, they are well on the way to achieving a feeling of importance.

In most cases attaining a sense of importance means also

the attaining of security. Security, particularly in the case of the adopted child, means the fulfillment of his wishes for prestige, that is, the acceptance of himself by his family and playmates as well as the achievement of self-respect. Security also means the child's being able successfully to use his powers, skills and abilities for interpersonal goals within the range of his interests.

For the adopted child attaining a sense of importance also means self-realization. By self-realization is meant a child's use of his talents, skills and powers to his own satisfaction within the realm of his own freely established sense of values. It also means the ability to reach out for and to find fulfillment of his needs for satisfaction and security in a socially accepted manner.

When a child has attained a sense of importance he has also attained a sense of self-esteem, security and ego-satisfaction. This is very important for the adopted child who usually lacks these.

In the adopted child the inculcation of a sense of importance goes a long way in overcoming his feelings of inferiority, jealousy and envy. In his case, the importance of feeling important is necessary for the following reasons:

1. An adopted child's satisfaction and happiness depend to a great extent upon his feeling of importance. By feeling important he is able to overcome his feeling of inferiority because of his adopted status.

2. His importance means that his foster parents esteem and love him. By feeling important he develops those qualities which justify his importance.

3. Being important for the adopted child means a sense of fulfillment as a human being; a feeling of being a useful, significant human being; of being part of a living unit, the family; and of contributing to it, and of being appreciated for his efforts.

CHAPTER NINETEEN

The Impact of Parental Occupation
on the Child's Emotions

When a child has reached a certain age, usually about 12, he becomes very much interested in what his father does for a living. His father's occupation then assumes great significance, and depending upon that occupation, he may either be proud of his parent or greatly disturbed by the kind of work he does for a living. In many instances parental occupation is the mold for certain aspects of the child's behavior and emotional status.

In general, the father's occupation exerts a rather profound influence on the child's outlook. A child whose father's occupation failed to provide for his primitive needs, will, at later stages of development, tend to experience all complexities of the outside world as reverberations of the original frustrating parental behavior. Particularly will this be true whenever the connection between parental behavior and his own needs and actions lacks emotional logic for the child.

The work that a child's father does assumes personal meaning to the child only as it acquires direct bearing on the child's immediate welfare. This is true in the early years of the child's life. However, when he grows older, the meaning of the different occupations of his friends' fathers and the occupation of his own father begins to take on cultural significance.

A child whose father is a lawyer is prouder of his father

than a child whose father is a day laborer. A child whose father is a peddler is more apt to regard his father with disdain than a child whose father is a famous novelist. Social prestige means a great deal to children, and the work the father does either gives prestige or denies it. Children who cannot attain significance and importance by their own actions obtain it through the occupations of their fathers. A child whose father has a position in the community to which prestige, fame or social approval is given feels more important than a child whose father works at some occupation which either sounds ridiculous to other children, or which lacks even a vestige of social acceptance.

The influence of the culture on the child's evaluation of his father's occupation is most obvious where the occupation gives the father special prerogatives. In such a case the child is able to bask in the reflected glory of his father's special powers and privileges. The child whose father's work is such that he is under constant pressure from his superiors, carrying out orders instead of giving them, tends to feel insecure and inferior himself. He is very likely to feel envious and jealous of children whose fathers have occupations which give them prestige, esteem and power.

There are instances in which the father feels uneasy about the social significance of his occupation, and this is conveyed to the child, who then also becomes emotionally upset about the kind of work his father is doing. There are cases in which the mother is not too pleased about her husband's occupation and tells him so. Their dissension is often conveyed to the child in such subtle ways that the child begins to feel insecure.

Parental dissension about the father's occupation may affect a child's way of life profoundly. For example, a woman may feel superior to her husband because of his coarseness and because of the crudeness of his occupation. His work is one that requires manual skill. His son, who has manual dexterity himself, develops the notion that this precludes achieving higher status and gives up learning altogether. He identifies himself with his father who does manual work. He also identifies himself with his mother who moves in circles which feel superior to manual laborers. He not only gives up all efforts at intellectual achievement, but also begins to fight society by delinquent actions.

What can be done to emotionally stabilize the child whose father's occupation makes him feel socially inferior and jealous of those children with fathers in positions of special prestige? The primary element to be considered is that these children are unduly sensitive in the way they react to their fathers' occupations. They are continually being handicapped by being over-sensitive. For the most part this sensitivity is expressed as vulnerability or as touchiness. The child who is unduly affected by parental occupation is as a rule more impressible than other children and this impressibility leads to sensitivity and a great deal of mental and emotional anguish which, of course, is not in the least necessary.

Every child feels frustrated at times because of different situations. Most children are able to take frustration. The unduly sensitive child who is constantly preoccupied with the fact that his father's work is not as important as that of the fathers of his friends, cannot cope adequately with his feelings of frustration, jealousy and social inferiority. He is unhappy about a situation which he cannot control.

As a result of his sensitivity he becomes mistrusting. Because of his father's occupation he expects and detects disapproval from his playmates. He is almost painfully aware of the fact that he is the son of a butcher, or a shoemaker, or a common laborer. He cannot live in emotional rapport with his friends, although he would very much like to do so.

Touchiness is another form of sensitivity. A child whose father's work is of a menial nature may become touchy because of this. His touchiness gives him a feeling of inferiority and insecurity. He feels slighted and assumes that other children want to impress their superiority upon him. This he is not able or willing to accept.

Touchiness is not as dominating a personality trait as vulnerability is. The touchy child is more aggressive than the vulnerable one. Short indulgence in daydreaming is sometimes seen in which the touchy child fancies himself as superior and comforts his hurt pride with imagined situations in which his father has a position of great social prestige. In this way he is able to relieve his intolerable tensions.

What can be done about the child who is emotionally upset and who is touchy and sensitive because of his father's occupation? There are several things that can be done. He can improve his mental and emotional health by seeking after certain aims and assuming certain attitudes.

Sensitivity and emotional conflicts in such children can be overcome:

1. When such a child regards himself as an individual in his own right, who has confidence in himself and who is made to know his true worth, which depends not on his father, but on himself.

2. When he is made to accept, work with, and to a large extent enjoy other individuals, who accept him on his own merits, qualities and capabilities.

3. When he is taught how to carry on his work, play, and family life with confidence and enthusiasm and with a minimum of conflict, fear and hostility.

There are certain basic emotional needs which must be fulfilled in such a child. These are:

1. To be the object of affection, to be loved for what one is himself and not for what one's close relative is or does.

2. To assert oneself as an individual—independent in thought and action—and to be allowed to reach one's own

decisions and to participate when plans are being made of which the child is the object.

3. To identify and be like others; to be part of a group.

4. To match oneself intellectually and physically with the environment, and to master and comprehend it.

5. To be able to face reality and to make the best of every situation.

CHAPTER TWENTY

The Illegitimate Child

The child who is born into this world without his parents being married is stigmatized from the very beginning, not because of any fault of his own, but because of the indiscretion of his parents, and because society does not accept children born out of wedlock. The illegitimate child has many difficulties to face and overcome simply because of the nature of his origin.

It is now generally conceded that for the normal development of a child, the presence and influence of both his parents is equally necessary. While the need for the mother is peremptory and immediate, the father does not enter into the child's life until consciousness develops sufficiently for the meaning of home and family to be grasped. When this stage is reached, the absence of the father or suitable father substitutes leaves the child without an important balancing influence. When the child reaches an age of awareness he has a need for authority. He needs to respect and obey, to be told what is right and what is wrong. The boy needs to look up to the father and to aspire to become like his father. The father should be a pillar of strength and a hero ideal for children of both sexes.

In the case of illegitimate birth the child's reactions to life are bound to be not completely normal. To be fatherless is difficult enough, but to be fatherless with the stigmata of illegitimate birth is quite unbearable. He feels himself to be under a constant handicap not of his own doing and about which he can do nothing. He feels himself to be the victim of an injustice beyond his control.

The illegitimate child feels out of place in the social scheme of things. He feels that he does not belong. The child's quest is to be accepted, to belong unquestionably. Emotional satisfaction is derived when the child has an un-doubted feeling that he is part of the world about him. The child has an inborn capacity to relate to the father and by identification to experience the emotional things of life which make us all human beings, capable of loving and of being loved, and of taking an active or creative part in social experiences. The illegitimate child is usually denied this.

The child born out of wedlock in time develops feelings of inferiority, inadequacy and shame together with feelings of envy and jealousy. He is extremely jealous of children who have the love and protection of both parents, while he lacks these. He feels insecure and isolated. He feels insecure because he finds himself in a situation different from that of his playmates.

The illegitimate child feels most acutely that he is not loved and appreciated as other children are. He feels that he is living in a vacuum, alone, unwanted, rejected. He lacks love and does not know how to give love.

For the child born out of wedlock love is required to give him a feeling of being wanted and of belonging. The child needs love even more than the adult because he is more helpless and more plastic. Only by experiencing love can he learn what love is, and knowing love, return it and experience emotional satisfaction. When the illegitimate child has little love, he has of necessity to turn his love to himself. When this is the case he cannot acquire the habit of giving love to others, a socializing bond to his environment which is so important for his proper emotional development.

Quite often the child born out of wedlock becomes neurotic because he is denied love. He acquires peculiar mannerisms and behavior patterns. He becomes resentful and in more extreme cases delinquent.

For the illegitimate child to be loved means to be protected against anxiety, to have self-esteem and to feel that he has a place in society. Love to him means abolishing loneliness and the dreadful feeling of isolation, of not belonging to anyone, of living in an emotional vacuum. Love means a merging of the one who loves with the one who is loved, so that the self of one person includes the self of the other; that which is one's is also the other's. As a consequence of such merging there is a mutual and complete participation in various feelings. Love is the intimate togetherness of the parent and the child in the experience of we-ness (being one).

Love in the case of the illegitimate child has a widening and broadening influence on his personality development. It permeates his thoughts and actions. It gives an added dimension to his everyday life by its fulfilled restfulness.

In addition to love the emotional care of the child born out of wedlock requires a building up of his self-esteem and an awareness of himself as a worthwhile individual. He must be so managed that he builds up an alive interest and awareness in everything and everyone. He must be given a mature and independent outlook. He must be made not to feel in constant need of protection. It should not be necessary for him to crave a constant demonstration that he is loved. He must be taught to tolerate disappointment.

Such a child should be taught that all his desires cannot be gratified at all times. He must find his greatest joy in being useful and helpful. He must be taught to get along with other people and not be unduly demanding. He must be able to meet his disappointments without attacks of rage, tantrums and sulking.

For the illegitimate child mental health means the avoidance of unnecessary conflict. To avoid conflict means to become well adjusted within himself and to his surroundings. He must learn to absorb emotional shocks. When this is done he can live with some degree of contentment and happiness.

CHAPTER TWENTY-ONE

The Minority Group Child

The child who is discriminated against because he belongs to a minority group is subjected to rather marked emotional tensions and conflicts. One of the distressing ideas he acquires is that a human being is not a human being as such. The minority group child is constantly being subjected to prejudice and discrimination in many different forms and he reacts to these with frustration, feelings of inferiority and jealousy.

One of the most serious forms of discrimination that the minority group child encounters is that of segregation in school. There is very little doubt that school segregation leads to an emotional conflict in the child's mind. It is apparently inevitable that this conflict arises in one form or another, and the conflict itself seems beyond solution.

The emotional conflict engendered by school segregation is a starting point of emotional instability or emotional illness. In many cases it results in severe feelings of isolation, of being different, of being an outcast, of not being a complete human being. Discrimination leads to emotional insecurity, to feelings of inferiority, to confusion and doubts.

The discriminated child makes all kinds of attempts, for the most part unconscious, to solve the conflict in his mind. He may seek to work out a realistic rationalization which would enable him to accept the facts, harsh and disagreeable as they are. This seldom works. He may make various attempts at repression. To do this successfully is not possible, for he is constantly faced with the urgent reality of the situation. Repression may spread to other areas. Overcompensation in one form or another is sometimes tried. The child may endeavor to obtain complete identification with children of a group not discriminated against. This is not possible. The result is that the child of the minority group feels stigmatized without being able to overcome the stigma by any efforts of his own. The result is frustration, envy and jealousy.

School segregation is only one aspect of discrimination that the minority group child has to face. There are others that he comes in contact with constantly in his daily life. He cannot go to restaurants or theatres, unless there are special places where he can sit. He cannot join social groups and clubs with children of the majority groups.

The sum total of feeling experienced is that he is being punished, not for anything wrong that he has done, but simply because of what he is, a child of a minority group.

Discrimination against the child in a minority group generates anxiety. They are in constant doubt about their place in society, in the community as a whole. They feel like second-class citizens, denied the rights of other children. They learn by heart the social ethics taught them in school, but they come against exactly the opposite in everyday life. They acquire the notion that it does not make much difference what they do—they are being punished for what they are and what their parents are.

A child in a minority group has a tendency to self-doubt and a heightening of tension with regard to all human relationships. He is taught in school about freedom of religion, freedom of speech, free education for all colors and creeds. But in reality these mean nothing as far as he is concerned.

He feels out of the scheme of things, isolated, outcast and alone. He reacts with frustration.

Frustration refers to the blocking of some aroused need or drive in which the satisfaction of the drive is interfered with, or is not available. Frustration implies the presence of some sort of barrier, and for the child of a minority group there are a great many social and psychological barriers.

The most common and direct response to frustration is aggression. All frustration leads to aggression unless this aggression is modified to some other response. There is no doubt that the primitive responses to frustration are various forms of aggression, which represent an effort on the part of the child to circumvent the barrier in order to obtain satisfaction. This primitive method of meeting frustration may be contrasted with the adjustive method of exploration and manipulation accompanied by learning. A young child who is unable to reach a coveted object may show his irritation at not being able to reach, and cry so as to bring assistance from another person; or he may proceed to explore possible ways of reaching the object through trial and error or insightful behavior. If his efforts are successful, he will have learned to meet frustration in a similar adaptive fashion on another occasion.

There are other substitutive methods of meeting frustration. One common method is by withdrawing and giving up the attempt to surmount the barrier. This may often be accompanied by fantasy in which success is achieved in the imagination. Neurotic behavior represents other types of responses which attempt to gain satisfaction of the thwarted drive by substitutive methods.

Frustration is a necessary experience in the life of every child, but in the case of the child in a minority group this is even more so. In ordinary cases frustration may lead to learning ways of overcoming the conditions causing frustration, when the conditions are reasonable. However, in cases of discrimination, the conditions are far from reasonable, and the frustration seems too formidable to surmount.

The discriminated against child is not only frustrated but subjected to other feelings as well. He is insecure; he feels that he cannot attain the goals that children of majority groups can. He is under a constant handicap because of his race, creed or color. This he feels is unfair, because it is something not of his own doing. In many cases this may lead to aggressive behavior.

In this case aggression is used to wrest satisfaction from the outside world. Aggression is the most primitive and universal response to frustration. There are three kinds of frustrations which normally lead to aggression. First, deprivation or unfulfilled desire; second, interference with or without restriction of activity; and third, an attack from the outside world which threatens bodily or psychological harm. Aggression is also conditioned by insecurity. Aggression may also be an outcome of feelings of inferiority, inadequacy and jealousy, and these are common feelings of a child in a minority group.

Prejudice is a serious social problem and its effects are widespread in our culture. Its effects on the child in a minority group are quite marked and serious. The child feels that he is being made an outcast for no good and sufficient reason, and that he can do nothing about it.

What can be done to help the child who is being discriminated against simply because he is a member of a minority group? He can be made to feel that he is a worthy member of a worthy race in spite of blind and unreasoning stupidity. He can be told the history of his race, and stories of the great men and women of his race who contributed to the progress of mankind. He can be taught to fight to overcome the obstacles put in his way, and that fighting to overcome them will make him a more worthwhile person for doing so. He can be made to feel that discrimination is simply an expression of inferiority, stupidity and fear on the part of the one who shows this discrimination, and that the one who is being discriminated against is a more socially mature and valuable member of society than the individual who does the discriminating.

CHAPTER TWENTY-TWO

The Neglected Twin

When there are identical twins and one is more favored than the other, feelings of resentment, envy and jealousy are very likely to develop in the twin who is less favored. It is a situation which is quite unique: one personality being divided into two, with one part favored, admired, catered to, and the other disregarded, passed over and more or less neglected. In the case of identical twins the neglected twin is more likely to be jealous than were there several years difference in age between two members of the same family. The more nearly alike the ages of the siblings, the greater the feelings of resentment and jealousy are likely to be. The closer in age the siblings are, the greater the jealousy of the less favored one.

The neglected twin does not receive any or as much praise and appreciation for his efforts as the favored one. His work is passed by, his presence is more or less ignored. He does not receive as much affection and attention. In a general sort of way both twins have developed to the same point of maturity. They use the same words and phrases to express themselves. Their emotional stature and their intelligences are equal. They do the same things, have the same opinions and yet one is favored and the other neglected. The rejected twin knows that he is the same as his brother, and yet he is not favored as much. This is a source of pronounced bewilderment, jealousy and resentment.

The favored twin in time acquires greater confidence, greater independence, a greater sense of inner strength than the less favored one who becomes shy, resentful, frustrated, unwanted and quite unhappy.

When any length of time elapses in the case of identical twins being treated differently, one being neglected and the other favored, the neglected twin will become grouchy, sullen, grasping, quarrelsome, jealous and disobedient, while the favored one will become bold and selfish, and in a very short time will acquire an exaggerated opinion of himself. When they are treated alike they behave alike. The capacity for equal happiness and equal ability in response to equal treatment is quite impressive in the case of identical twins. All children want to be happy; they all want to succeed. They respond eagerly to any opportunity.

The case of the neglected twin is an all too common one. The solution is not difficult. No problem can be treated in isolation, and anyone working with children makes the point that children, not problems, are treated. A specific attack on the problem is required in this case, as in others in which children are involved.

In the case of the neglected twin, the specific attack is to remove the cause, and that is to treat both twins alike. The earlier this is done the better will be the results.

However, when the neglected twin has been subjected to neglect for some time a different situation exists and the solution of the problem is not quite as easy. He must be re-educated and reoriented. Re-education involves the substitution of effective methods of meeting the problem for the present ineffective ones. The neglected twin must be taught to try new experiences, set new goals, and achieve new satisfactions from socially desirable behavior. As in any educative process, the child must actively participate, rather than passively do what is suggested to him. He should be encouraged to think things through critically, make plans to improve, and be encouraged to achieve inner satisfaction in spite of any hindrances and emotional handicaps that are put in his path.

Any method by which the child can express his emotional feelings usually results in at least a temporary release of tension. He may do so by overt action or by verbal means, and he may be conscious or not of what he is doing. The value of this method lies in the fact that the child clarifies his feelings by verbalizing them, and gains a release from tension which makes it possible to face the real situation more constructively.

Emotional behavior is usually characterized by confused thinking, especially with regard to one's own position in the situation. Once the individual has things straight, much of the emotion is apt to disappear. Putting events in their proper relationship, reducing exaggerations, putting emphasis on positive qualities—these are part of the process of reorienting the neglected twin.

Parental attitude is of great importance in the lives of all children. Competition between parents for the affection of the favored twin leads to pronounced feelings of neglect and rejection on the part of the unfavored twin. When the favored twin receives toys and other manifestations of favoritism while the neglected one receives nothing, a source of extreme tension is created which may in time lead to behavior disturbances.

Children respond to the attitudes of their parents in a variety of ways. They become more or less aggressive to the extent that they are frustrated by their parents, either by control which is too severe, or by fear of loss of their parents' love. Both of these attitudes are variations of parental rejection.

The neglected twin may develop psychopathic tendencies —that is, a social behavior without the usual feelings of guilt and conscience which most children have when they have done wrong—when parental control and direction are inadequate.

Feelings of inadequacy or of inferiority and inadequacy are traceable to the attitudes that parents take toward them. The parent who admires the child and speaks well of it is helping the child to think well of itself, whereas the child who receives constant criticism or reproach and the threat of loss of love is the one who is tormented by feelings of inadequacy, envy and jealousy.

Social characteristics are determined by early parent-child relationships, which help determine whether the child will later be friendly or unfriendly, honest or dishonest, truthful and untruthful. The less favored twin will develop the less desirable social attitudes.

The attitudes of parents toward their children owe their origin to personality factors which the parents bring with them from their own earlier childhood experiences. It has been found, for instance, that the attitude which the parent adopts toward a child is frequently a displacement of the attitude which had been held earlier toward the parent's own parents or to his siblings. The father, for instance, may display to his son the same hostility which he had shown at an earlier age toward his own father, but never thoroughly worked through. In the second place, parental attitudes toward their children are projections onto the child of attitudes which the parent unconsciously holds toward himself. If a parent feels guilty and unworthy, rather than admit these feelings himself, he may project them onto his child, and be extremely harsh and punitive for characteristics in the child which he is unable and unwilling to recognize in himself.

In undesirable parental-children relationships, the faults are quite often those of the parents. The parents must be educated along the proper lines to treat their children in the proper way.

The relations between parent and child are not necessarily determined by the personality of the parent but are always susceptible of becoming constructive under the proper guidance. Every child has the possibility of growing up in an atmosphere of security and encouragement.

CHAPTER TWENTY-THREE

The Only Child

Being an only child may have its advantages, but there are certain disadvantages as well. The problems of the only child may be no different from those of any other child, but occasionally they are exaggerated by the concentrated solicitude of the family, or the lack of opportunity to share, not only belongings, but also the time and interest of the grown-ups. The only child is often a lonely child, a child who is envious and jealous of children who have brothers and sisters to share their lives and interests.

Parents of only children should be keenly aware of the importance of providing opportunities for companionship and sharing. When this is done, the only child will learn the value of co-operative living with others. The only child may become a selfish child when opportunities for sharing with others are denied him.

The disadvantage of being an only child accrues from the fact that the only child quite often becomes the center of attraction. He becomes dependent, inadequate, self-centered; he may acquire all sorts of behavior peculiarities, such as refusing to sleep alone, becoming finicky about his food, particular about his companions, snobbish, with a tendency to regard himself as the center of his own little universe—his family.

The only child quite often does not know the need of sharing with other children. It is axiomatic that children need the companionship of those their own age, as one of the first lessons in how to live in this world. Relatedness with others is the first great lesson of interpersonal relationship, and this must be acquired early in life in order for a person to function as an effective social unit.

The only child should be taught quite early the joy of sharing. Greediness, acquisitiveness for selfish purposes, hoarding toys, always receiving instead of giving, are apt to become characteristic of the only child if measures are not taken to prevent this. There is a need in the expanding personality of the child to try its power by saying "NO," when it is easier to say "YES."

The only child is more likely to get bored, and when a child gets bored, all sorts of mischief may result. When a child's abilities are never challenged by something that takes real effort to accomplish, he is apt to fall into slovenly habits of working and thinking. It is easy to be spoiled when one is the only child, and that makes it harder to realize the needs and rights of others. When an important problem in life presents itself the only child may resent it because of the time and effort it involves.

The only child is more likely than others to become dependent and lack self-reliance. For him, therefore, the inculcation of self-reliance is most important. The achievement of self-reliance is an important aspect of growing up, more so for the only child than for others.

Since home training appears to be so important in the development of self-reliance, the question of the generality or specificity of the trait takes on real practical significance. If self-reliance is a single, general trait, to train a child to be self-reliant in certain typical situations would tend to make him self-reliant in all kinds of situations. If on the other hand, self-reliant behavior is specific to every situation, to train a child to be self-reliant in feeding himself, for example, would have no effect upon his behavior in a somewhat different situation, such as getting dressed in the morning.

This question has scarcely been raised at all in the past.

It has been assumed that self-reliance is a single, general character trait. Recent studies, however, suggest that this is not the case. There are at least four or five, or possibly more, distinct and relatively independent kinds of self-reliance, each functioning in a particular area of human activity. Self-reliance, then, does not appear to be specific to each particular activity. Instead there are perhaps as many "traits" of self-reliance as there are distinct types of everyday life situations or distinct areas of activity in which the child might either depend upon himself or be irresponsible and dependent upon others in meeting the situation.

Life is a series of situations in which personal problems must be solved, difficulties and dilemmas faced and resolved, and decisions made. If a child manages as a rule to get himself out of difficult situations; if he habitually faces alone his personal problems such as choosing an article of clothing; if he usually seems to know what to do in a difficult situation; if he can make up his mind without difficulty; and if he is willing to take the consequences of his own decisions, he is self-reliant, mature and independent. He has learned how to stand on his own two feet and act on his own responsibilities in regard to personal problems and difficulties.

Another activity area in which self-reliant behavior might be seen in some children is that of ordinary daily work and the use of time. If a child has so many things which he likes to do that he never has the time to feel bored when thrown upon his own resources; if he enjoys working out new ways of doing his daily tasks; if he is conscientious in the performance of his share of the work and even is likely to go ahead with additional work on his own responsibility; and if he is never at a loss to know what to do for his own entertainment, he is certainly self-reliant. In this case, however, his self-reliance involves industriousness and a sort of resourcefulness in work. It is self-reliance in work and the use of time.

A third group of situations in which a rather distinct variety of self-reliance might manifest itself consists of those in which person-to-person relationships are especially involved. The child who has learned to assume the responsibility of getting himself ready and off to school on time; who dislikes to be late for any appointment and has formed the habit of seeing to it that he keeps his appointments and promises; and who is able to feel confident at examination time because he has on his own responsibility kept up in his studies, this child is definitely self-reliant. He is self-reliant in the sense of meeting his obligations to others—in keeping up his end generally in his relationships with them. He has learned through experience that irresponsible behavior in such matters usually brings unpleasant consequences. He has also learned that by keeping his word and remembering his obligations, his personal dealings with others consistently bring satisfaction to himself. This variety of self-reliance might be called personal responsibility.

Children show varying degrees of self-reliance in still another type of situation—the group situation. When small groups form for play and other activities, certain children assume leadership, others make contributions to the group thinking and action, and still others are merely passive followers or non-participants. At least part of this variability in behavior is due to individual differences in self-reliance —a resourcefulness in group situations.

The child who is well developed in this trait is usually the one who is asked to plan special events at school. He is usually ready with ideas and suggestions on such occasions and those suggestions are usually practical and usable for the occasion. This sort of self-reliance, then, especially involves resourcefulness and a certain sort of aggressiveness together with dependability and willingness to work in group situations.

Each of these varieties of self-reliance is relatively independent of the others. The development of each in a given child depends upon experience in a particular type of life situation. The implications of this in child training are clear. If a child is to become self-reliant and independent in meeting and solving his own personal problems, he must be given opportunities for practice and responsibility appropriate to his age and ability, and always with guidance, in actually making his own decisions. If he is to become self-reliant and resourceful in work and in the use of his time, he must learn by actual experience, among other things, that to do the little tasks assigned to him conscientiously and with dispatch means more time for the activities he enjoys. If he is to learn to rely upon himself in fulfilling his obligations, doing his part and in general maintaining satisfactory personal relations with others, again to his appropriate degree, he as a child must be put upon his own responsibility in fulfilling his part of the bargain with those about him. And finally, if he is to develop self-reliance and resourcefulness in group situations, he must have actual experience as a child in participating in group activities. He must be given ample opportunity and encouragement to express his ideas and at the same time be made to feel that those ideas are given weight and consideration. The family meal provides a very favorable natural setting for experience and development of this sort.

The democratic home atmosphere provides greatest opportunity for the development of the various kinds of self-reliant behavior. Studies show that children of parents who believe in strict and autocratic parental control are, on the average, less self-reliant than children whose parents do not hold such beliefs. Self-reliance in all its aspects is best developed in a family atmosphere of mutual confidence, affection, companionability, where many group activities both in and outside the home are planned and enjoyed together. This is especially important in the case of the only child.

CHAPTER TWENTY-FOUR

The Step-child

The step-child has rather special problems of his own; he has lost a parent and he has gained another parent—a step-mother or a step-father. He finds it necessary to adjust to new conditions. How well he will adjust is dependent upon several factors, and among the most important of these is age. Ordinarily an infant will effectuate a satisfying relationship more readily than an adolescent. When the child is young, pliable, and sufficiently dependent to feel the need of someone to caress and fondle him, and help him with his troubles, he will adjust quite readily to his step-mother.

The younger a child is, the more helpless he is, and the more he craves affection and mothering. He cannot live happily without such attention. It is a necessary part of his growth and development. If he receives the affection he craves, he is quite willing to accept a substitute parent with fewer reservations than an older child. An older child has too many memories, and, if they are pleasant ones of a mother or father who has departed, he is still attached to them, and he cannot too easily forsake them. He will be more apt to consider the step-parent as an unwelcome intruder into the family circle. He will be resentful, distrustful and suspicious.

The step-parent's lot is also not a happy one. Oftentimes a stepmother finds a child of five or six rather difficult to manage. If he has been pampered by an over-indulgent aunt or grandmother, he may have developed habits which can be changed only with great difficulty. Mere youthfulness will not always assure a successful adjustment to a step-parent. There are quite a few other factors that enter into the situation. These are previous up-bringing, and physical, mental and emotional factors.

As the child grows older, the difficulties of adjusting to a new situation increase. This is particularly true when a substitute parent enters the picture. The child has already made adjustments to his own parent and has arrived at a more or less satisfactory situation; he is set in his ways and he has succeeded in adjusting himself to his family situation. With the arrival of a step-parent, he has to re-arrange his ways of living to suit his new parent, and the older the child is, the more difficult it is for him to do this.

When children are striving to attain a status of individuality and independence, it is particularly difficult to accept the added burden of a new family tie, which a step-parent engenders. A step-mother may earnestly desire to make a good home for her step-children, but, try as she may, she will find that in many ways her ideas and standards will differ from those to which the children have been accustomed. Rarely has she had anything to do with the upbringing and training of the children, and she has not had an opportunity to become familiar with their habits, ways of thinking, personalities and physical peculiarities. Had she been with the children from the time they were born, they could have gradually grown up together and things would certainly be easier. In addition, some step-mothers have had little experience in dealing with children. Even the most carefully thought out plans may become disrupted when one of them acquires an adolescent, particularly if he has been over-protected and over-indulged by some relative. She will have a very difficult time trying to undo the damage that has been done. No matter how skillful and patient she may be, she is already under a disadvantage because she is a step-parent and as such all her actions are suspect. Every move she makes is regarded with suspicion by the step-child, and the situation is a very difficult one.

It is not at all surprising that a child reveres and idealizes his departed parent, for, even though there are, without the least doubt, many good and worthy step-parents, he has a rather dubious chance of having a second home equally as good as the first one. The first of anything seems better and more desirable. If the mother has died and there are several children, a caretaker is undoubtedly required. A new factor has now entered into the picture. The father has a more restricted range of choice than he had before his first marriage. There are many women who will not want to take care of and bring up some other woman's children. He may make a good choice or a bad one. No one actually knows until the step-mother has entered into the family circle and begins to function as a substitute parent. She may have the intelligence and personality to be a good step-mother, or she may not. In some cases, there may be a poor beginning with subsequent improvement of the situation.

One of the most pressing problems a step-parent, especially a step-mother, must face is that of finding satisfactory roles for her step-children. If the children are no longer infants or very young, they have become accustomed to certain roles, and these cannot be disturbed with impunity. If a step-mother comes into a home and in her desire to institute a co-operative household assigns the task of washing dishes to an over-grown boy, athletically inclined, who regards such a task as a "sissy" one, she will get into difficulties. If she is wise and understanding she will study the personalities of her step-children, their desires and inclinations, and assign to each a task that they would like to do. She should make a serious attempt to find out what her step-children like most to do and assign such tasks to them. A little commonsense will go a long way in a situation of this kind.

The child's emotions are of the greatest importance in the family situation. Insecurity very often manifests itself in rivalry for affection. When a child feels uncertain and insecure, he may make a strong effort to get his full share, and quite often more, of affection. He will endeavor to keep to himself as much as possible the attention of his parent and resent bitterly sharing with one who is a newcomer into the family circle. Quite often a step-child feels that instead of having acquired a mother for himself, his father has acquired a wife with whom the child must share his father. It very often happens when there is a very close relationship between the child and real parent, that the child resents the coming of a step-parent and uses every endeavor to crowd out the newcomer.

When a child feels that he is being crowded out of the affections of a parent, he becomes resentful. If a step-mother comes in, it makes little difference how good she is. If the child feels that he is being crowded out of his father's affections, he will turn against the step-mother. In this instance, jealousy is a very important factor. The child is jealous of his father's affection and he feels that he cannot share it with anyone. Jealousy is also manifested when the father begins to show affection for the step-mother with apparent disregard for the child. Jealousy may become mingled first with envy and later with resentment.

There are times when a child may be rejected by the step-parent and then gradually rejected by the real parent. In order to hold the new mate, the parent will pay increasing attention to him and thus crowd the child out. Affection is withdrawn from the child and concentrated exclusively on the step-parent. This will intensify any feelings of jealousy and envy that may have existed only in slight degree.

Quite a few children have complained that the step-parent becomes the dominant and central person in the home and exerts undue influence on the real parent. When this is the case, the child is almost entirely left out of the family picture and he comes to feel that he is unwanted.

The status of a step-child is never quite a happy one at the outset. If a parent in a well-integrated family dies, the child loses a companion, a sympathetic friend, a guide and counselor, to whom he has been closely attached, and this quite often has a disastrous effect on the child. The orderly pattern of life in the home is often changed with rather unnerving abruptness, and the child is left emotionally adrift. He has the uncomfortable feeling that he no longer has a haven of security to which he may return with confidence after buffetings on the outside.

The step-child is often plagued with feelings of insecurity because of his situation. A feeling of insecurity may come in one of several ways. When a child considers that he is treated differently from others, he feels insecure. He does not know how to respond to an unpatterned situation, nor does he know how to adjust to it. When the step-parent treats the child differently than he has been treated by his real parent, he becomes bewildered. He feels that he is being singled out for special treatment not to his liking or under-standing. He feels somewhat stigmatized, somewhat different. This leads to insecurity intermingled with feelings of infe-riority and jealousy.

Sibling rivalry, particularly when favoritism is shown to a brother or sister, very often leads to feelings of insecurity and frustration. Quite often this may not be serious in an un-broken home, but in a home that has a step-parent, it may become a rather significant factor. When a child is born to this second union, it demands the greater portion of the mother's affection and attention, and the father also gives some of his time to the new arrival. Because this new child has two real parents while the step-child in the family has only one, the baby usually has certain advantages which tend to make the older child feel less important and for that reason less secure.

Quite often children apologize for the difference and even tell lies to conceal the fact that they have a step-parent. Because of the traditional attitude toward step-parents, and particularly toward the step-mother, the step-child often develops a sense of inferiority because he, unlike other children, has a substitute parent. Because of this, many children who acquire step-parents in infancy are not told about this. However, when they learn the true facts later on they experience some emotional shock and disappointment.

The step-child has special problems of his own to face and solve. He cannot do this alone without help from the adults in his family. Quite often just a little commonsense and ordinary consideration will go a long way to make his life less tense and stressful.

CHAPTER TWENTY-FIVE

The Jealous Child

The jealous child is not an uncommon phenomenon in our culture. The jealous child is rather frequently encountered because conditions in our society are such that childhood is not always the happy, carefree, secure existence it is popularly supposed to be. Jealousy is a manifestation of many inner needs that are not or cannot be fulfilled. In many instances, it is the final total result of physical, mental and emotional deficiencies of one sort or another.

Stated simply, a child is jealous when he wants something that someone else has and he has not. This something may be physical, mental, emotional, economic, social, financial, etc. Jealousy, when it is not exaggerated, is normal in children as it is in adults. A jealous child will not necessarily grow up to be a jealous adult. However, jealousy, although in itself only a symptom, can become harmful when it arouses marked disapproval in the parents, causing the child to feel wrong or bad. Parents need to understand what lies back of the child's behavior. They must learn how to help him accept his feeling of envy and jealousy without arousing a sense of guilt that may impede his progress toward full maturity. Many adults exhibit neurotic symptoms because of faulty handling of jealousy by parents when they were children.

Basically, it is the child's need for protection that makes him anxious to obtain and preserve his parents' affection, and it is this need that causes him to look with suspicion upon his brothers and sisters. According to Freudian think-ing, the jealousy of an only child takes the form of the Oedipus complex. Arrival of another child causes much resentment on the part of the first born, as he feels deprived of many of his privileges. Later, the addition of a third child may give him the opportunity to take his revenge. He may form a coalition with the youngest child against the second born, who is caught in the middle.

Jealousy between brother and sister is either based upon envy of anatomical and biological differences, or upon a mis-understanding of the differential treatment received during education.

An unusual situation arises when there are identical twins in the family. The twins regard themselves as a unit and are regarded as such by their brothers and sisters, who may look with envy at the special attention the pair receives. As the twins realize that the strength of their position rests upon their being alike, they become anxious to enhance and pre-serve this likeness as long as possible. Hatred and love exist in these families to the same extent as in others, and tension and confusion is said to be even greater where more sets of twins are present. Nonidentical twins usually take an indi-vidualistic attitude toward each other.

Death of a parent is a grievous blow to the child's feeling of security. It increases his dependency on the remaining parent, and makes him even more possessive of the parent and more jealous of his siblings. There is the danger that a widowed mother, occupied with her own grief and burdened with new responsibilities, may overlook the sorrows of her children.

If a home is broken by death or divorce the children may find new reasons for jealousy. They will oppose any wish of the parent to remarry, and should a remarriage take place, the step-parent becomes the object of jealousy. Should both partners bring their respective broods into the new household, the gates are opened wide for every form and current of envy, hatred and jealousy.

Jealousy is least developed in neglected children, simply because there is not much to be jealous of. This points to the paramount influence which the attitude of the parents exerts on the development of childhood jealousy, and thereby on the character formation of the child. Playing favorites, inconsistent discipline, overt comparison of the children—all will have a devastating effect on the children's state of mind. These practices will fan the flame of jealousy and create an exaggerated spirit of rivalry which later may result in an unsound search for power that can never be satisfied. The role of the parent should be that of a moderator. The children should not be told to "love" one another, as the competitive spirit cannot be eradicated completely from the family. It is the family that must prepare the child to live in our competitive society.

Jealousy is also aroused by social inequalities, by economic inequalities, by financial deficiencies. Children are quick to note and observe what other children have in the way of material goods, social security and position. When they find these things desirable in others, they also desire them for themselves, and when they lack these they become jealous.

Children also know the meaning of good health and physical perfection. They see them in other children, and when they lack these they are intensely jealous. Especially do they resent any illness which sets them apart from others, such as diabetes, epilepsy, tuberculosis; they resent any physical condition, such as harelip, facial and figure deformities, which tend to stigmatize them.

Jealousy is of instinctual origin. Its suppression would only drive it undercover and poison the child's mind. It should be brought into the open and managed with frankness and honesty. Only in this way are the avenues opened for the promotion of emotional maturity.

Parents must be equipped not only to recognize jealousy in their children, but also to cope with it. There are several good rules which should be kept in mind when parents deal with childhood difficulties of any kind. These are:

1. Don't rush.
2. Wise actions are based on facts.
3. Seek out the simplest explanations first.
4. Try the simplest remedies first.
5. Each situation should be handled on its individual merits.
6. Do not cling obstinately to a mode of handling that has proved ineffective, but do not rush about in a frenzied dash from one method to another.
7. Distinguish between the ostensible difficulty and the real one.
8. Prevention is better than cure.

It is desirable that parents become acquainted with some rather simple rules of mental hygiene in order to be in a better position to guide their children into the proper channels of effective living. The parents must be in sound mental and emotional health themselves for the child to develop into emotional maturity.

In a civilization such as our own in which the position of the child has been magnified out of all proportion to general family needs and functions, parents tend to compete for the major place in the child's affection. In order to win in this most undesirable type of competition the parents bribe the child by too many ill-considered gifts. Poor educational practice as well as poor emotional control develops from such a situation. Habits of emotional response are based on the wrong type of stimulation.

The child who looks forward to the coming of a loved one because he counts on presents from that individual develops a habit of giving affection only when paid to give it. Psychologically this is one of the most dangerous mental traits since the satisfaction of affection by the response which comes from the loved object is the desired end, not the amount which one can cajole or demand from that loved object. Not only will poor habit patterns be substituted for more desirable ones but the whole security of the child will be interfered with. Young children are secure when the parents obviously love each other and have confidence in each other. For one parent to question another upsets young children. For one parent to criticize another or quarrel with another is disturbing in proportion to the seriousness of the quarrel. Competition for the affection of the child involves both quarreling and questioning. Not only is this true, but in order to secure the affection of the child each parent attempts to break down the discipline enforced by the other.

Many parents, either because of pride in the child or because they feel that unusual success or achievement on the part of children reflects glory on the parent, try to force children beyond the limits of their age and physical strength or beyond their intelligence level. There is no factor more productive of insecurity and resulting behavior problems than the feeling that the individual can never live up to what is asked of him. In infancy the parents may try to force the child to talk. They may work for hours until the child flies into a temper tantrum or drops into a sound sleep to protect himself from a world in which he is not succeeding. Parents attempt to teach children the names of colors one, two or even three years ahead of the time when names of colors are learned normally. They try to teach him to be polite long before the concept of politeness is developed.

At school they try to push their children more than a year beyond their chronological and mental level or try to force them to achieve grades which are beyond their capacities. If the father or mother has been a leading student, all of the children in the family must also be leading students. If the father or mother has been brilliant in mathematics, economics, science, or any other activity, all the children of the family must be brilliant and to an equal degree. Even the most superficial knowledge of the transmission of hereditary capacities would make it clear that no such equal inheritance by all of the children is possible. Parents should reconcile themselves to the fact that their children will not be alike and that they will not inherit parental characteristics to an equal degree. Even identical quadruplets are not identical in appearance and capacities though they are similar.

A third area in which parents attempt to force children to accept patterns which they cannot approximate, is the attempt to make their children carry out all the ambitions not realized in their own early childhood and youth. All of these attempts to dominate the child and force him into a pattern which is not his own tend to result in behavior problems of all degrees of seriousness. In infancy and early childhood they are almost always productive of problems in the field of three habits which have a psychological basis, namely eating, sleeping and toilet habits. They may also produce such behavior problems as stubbornness, temper tantrums and general emotional instability; and may also result in defiance of authority, which in later years may be transferred to authority in general almost in the same degree in which the earlier authority of the dominating parents was rejected.

There is nothing more productive of difficulty of every kind than the feeling by the child that he is not wanted. Many parents develop this feeling in children through thoughtlessness or through injudicious teasing. There are also parents who actually do not wish to have children or did not wish to have this child at this particular time or who felt that they already had a sufficient number of children before this child was born. Immediately after birth the child is aware that his parents do not wish to have him. Every individual needs the feeling that his family wants him, that he is accepted and that no one can take his place. If there are two boys in the family and a third boy is born, it is often necessary to assure him that he is wanted and that his parents were not wishing for a girl, when he was born. If on the other hand the family is all girls it is frequently necessary to assure one or all of them that the family wanted them. A child who feels that he is not wanted will, either because of general insecurity or resentment, find out what disturbs the parents most and repeat this behavior indefinitely. The fact that children are capable of muscle reading probably accounts for their ability to find out which behavior is the most disturbing.

Parents who have no deep and satisfying relationship between themselves are apt to seek in the parent-child relationship all of those satisfactions which would have been possible had they had a normal husband-wife relationship. They call the child by the names which lovers use for each other. They fondle and kiss their children and even use their children as an outlet for their feelings.

In a good family relationship the affection between the mother and father transcends all of the affectional relationships between the parents and their children. This is the best type of family relationship inasmuch as children who feel a strong and steady affection between their parents are themselves secure. Parents may make many mistakes in discipline and in other respects, and yet the child will develop few or no behavior problems, if the love relationship between the parents themselves and between the parents and their children is normal, strong and steady. This is the first prerequisite to a secure childhood.

The old form of patriarchal civilization made it possible for a large number of individuals within the family to remain children emotionally. Many of them remained in the stage of self-fixation characteristic of the child under six months of age. Some remained fixated on their parents, either the mother or father. Others remained in the gang stage in which the highest emotional satisfactions are received only as a member of a crowd.

Since the patriarchal period has just passed there are many parents who are immature. Immaturity on the part of the parent makes him behave toward and with the child as a child with other children. When the three-year-old disobeys, he and the parents "fight it out." In fact, their whole relationship from birth to maturity or until the child becomes more mature than the parent will be that of quarreling children. Children need beyond anything else to count on the fact that their parents are wise as well as kind. They need to feel the protection of individuals older, as well as wiser and more mature than themselves. Where this is lacking all sorts of fears develop. These may even lead to an anxiety neurosis.

As experience in child guidance accumulates, the development of personality is seen more and more to be the direct result of parent-child relations. There seem to be periodic shifts in the emphasis given to nature or nurture in explaining the antecedents of personality and the process of development. The discoveries of the great biologists of the nineteenth century indicated the mechanisms of biological inheritance, and at the beginning of the present century it was fashionable to speak of instincts and to look to heredity as an explanation of personality. But clinical and experimental studies of growth in infancy show that much of personality is molded by the early experiences of the child, and that the most important of these experiences cluster about the relations between parent and child.

Some have argued that parent-child relations cannot possibly account for even a small part of the development of personality of children. The argument runs that in the same family the environment is to all intents and purposes the same; therefore, differences in the personality of the children must be largely attributable to heredity. However, that children in the same family are in the same environment is a gratuitous assumption. Close observation would indicate that parents respond to each child in the family differently, according to the age, sex, order of birth, and physical and mental characteristics. It would seem as though each child plays a unique role with regard to the parents' needs, and thereby assumes a different relationship to his parents.

Parent-child relationships have at least two dimensions—the demand on parents for security and for authority. These two aspects of parent-child relationships are frequently in conflict. Both of these demands are important. The first is basic in the establishment of sound emotional attitudes; the second helps the child grow into adult society. Many parents have difficulty in their authority relationships with their children. They complain that the children are disobedient, disrespectful, stubborn and resistant, and react poorly to discipline. Not infrequently a parent of a young child will visit the nursery school and observe the methods used successfully by a teacher, but will fail in an attempt to apply these same methods at home. The difficulty here arises in the fact that parents and children are emotionally involved with each other, and that it is extremely difficult for a parent to use the methods of the school with the same impartial objectivity. Because their relationship is one to which they respond with considerable emotion, many parents find that they cannot give a child a feeling of emotional security when it becomes necessary for them to exert their authority.

Parental attitudes toward children are difficult to study by the usual methods of psychological inquiry and observation. It is next to impossible for an outside observer to learn what goes on in the bosom of the family. Parents do not wish to reveal their faults to the outside world, and their relationships with their children are impeccable when they may be under public scrutiny. Parents best display their true attitudes and feelings on getting up in the morning, during the period of dressing, at the time of going to bed, and also at meal time. It is for this reason that ordinary reports on parent-child relationships are untrustworthy. A mother may have the reputation of being extremely devoted to her children because when friends and relatives are present, she expresses herself most affectionately; whereas in the intimacy of the family she may express hatred and intolerance.

The principal elements in parent-child relationships are:
1. Love and hatred.
2. Control and authority.
3. Punishment.
4. Neglect.
5. Elevation or depression of the child's ego.
6. Parental anxiety.
7. Projection of parental ambition on the child.
8. Various combinations of parental attitude.

Most of the foregoing discussion is in terms of parent behavior and attitude toward children. Perhaps parent-child relationships have their most fundamental character in the feelings of the parent, whether they be love or hatred. The casual observer probably believes that mother love is the normal and typical attitude of the parent toward the child. The degree to which parents hate their children is probably not commonly appreciated. In child guidance clinics it is very common for parents to express negative feelings toward their children. While it might be expected that parents whose children present problems might exhibit negative feelings, evidence is accumulating that every parent on some occasions and to some degree feels annoyed and out of patience with his child. When this attitude tends to outweigh the love feelings of the parent toward the child, it is called rejection. The course of the parent's feeling toward the child is all-important in determining the child's emotional security and in influencing the development of personality. All the evidence points to the fact that genuine love by the parent gives the child security and helps the child to develop a stable and socialized character; whereas parent hatred encourages instability, and leads to unsocial behavior.

Parents also vary in degree and mode of the control and authority which they wield. On the one hand, there is the parent who exercises no control and gives the child complete freedom. At the other extreme is the parent who exercises a high degree of restrictive authority. Neither of these two extremes is best for child development. The child who suffers from too great laxness in parental authority will fail to learn the behavior expected by society, while the child who is under too great parental control may either develop resentment and hostility to authority, or become extremely docile, submissive and subservient. The best results are obtained by a judicious mixture of granting the child freedom and exercising firmness when the occasion demands.

A third variable in parent-child relationships is punishment. A certain amount of punishment is inevitable in the control of the child. Even though this may be very mild and on the whole benign, in psychological experiments merely saying the word "wrong" to a subject has been termed punishment, and any method by which the parent shows his displeasure with the child and which causes the child pain (physical or mental) may act in the nature of punishment. In general, it is agreed that, while punishment is sometimes necessary in order to protect the child from danger, on the whole punitive parent-child relationships are not constructive; and that children develop more satisfactorily under the stimulus of encouragement than they do under the inhibiting influence of punishment.

A fourth variable in parent-child relationships is the tendency to give the child care and attention, on the one hand, and to neglect the child on the other. Here, too, a middle ground is preferable. Children can be harmed by oversolicitude on the part of the parents who, by depriving their child of normal frustrations, keep him infantile and fail to offer sufficient stimulus to development. On the other hand, the rejecting mother who neglects her child is threatening his emotional security, and this attitude is likely to arouse traits of aggression and hostility.

The fifth variable in parent-child relationships is the tendency of the parent to elevate or depreciate the child's ego. On the one hand, the parent can praise the child and show his pleasure in and appreciation of the child's performance and achievement. On the other hand, the parent may severely criticize the child and depreciate his accomplishments. The best results in child development are to be found in an atmosphere of encouragement and appreciation.

The sixth variable in the parent's attitude towards the child may be found in the parent's tendency toward anxiety. The stable parent will have a stabilizing effect on the child. The anxious parent, on the other hand, will communicate his anxiety to the child, and will tend to make the child fearful or inhibited.

The seventh factor which is frequently found in the parent's attitude toward the child is the projection of the parent's own ambitions on the child. A parent frequently is disappointed in fulfilling some of his childhood ambitions. He may have been unable to go as far as he wished in school, or have been thwarted in his social or love relationships. Perhaps he has failed to climb as high as he aspired on the vocational ladder. Parents sometimes attempt to realize these unfulfilled hopes by projecting their ambitions onto their children. If this is done in the spirit of encouragement without too much pressure, the results may be constructive. On the other hand, if parents attempt to force a child to achieve their goals, it may result in the loss of the child's ambition and his adoption of an attitude of indifference.

These attitudes may be present in different combinations. One parent, for instance, may exercise strict control of a child, while the other parent is lenient. One parent may be extremely punitive, while the other parent is affectionate and reassuring. Children almost inevitably suffer from inner conflicts when there is a conflict in the attitudes with which they are treated by their parents.

These attitudes on the part of the parents may also vary in the way in which they are openly or subtly expressed. It is a common state of affairs for the parent to feel underlying hatred and hostility toward the child which arouses the parent's guilt. Since no one wishes to think of himself as a bad parent, these hostile feelings are partially repressed, and the parent adopts an overt attitude of overprotection and overindulgence toward the child. The child responds to the repressed as well as to the expressed attitude. Overprotection or overindulgence usually contains the hostility as well as the professed feeling of love. A parent may confine a child by so many restrictions in the name of health and safety as to severely deprive the child of freedom in other ways and make life miserable for him. Overindulgence as a way of being good to the child may harm the child by making it difficult for him to mature or by causing him to adopt antisocial ways.

Children vary in the development of independence and self-reliance. On the one hand, parents who are overprotective and oversolicitous of their children may hedge them in with so many precautions and do so much for them that they prevent them from growing up and developing properly. Children who have developed the greatest amount of independence and self-reliance are usually those who are given considerable amounts of freedom of action coupled with support when needed.

Parent-child relationships are responsible for fears and tendencies to be withdrawn and seclusive. These tendencies may be a response to the lack of security in the parent-child relationships, and also, in part, to extremes in parental control and authority. Children may respond to the dominating parent with fear and seclusiveness, but they may also respond in similar fashion to an inadequate amount of parental control.

Discipline is a very important factor in the upbringing of children. Discipline is a process of training and learning that encourages growth and development. Parents should attempt to help their children learn a way of life that leads to usefulness and happiness. Parents should teach by precept and example, and their children should learn by imitation and practice. It should be emphasized that discipline does not mean punishment nor the idea of punishment. Discipline means observing and adhering to the rules of life.

Parents make a child happy or unhappy by their degree of understanding and acceptance of his intelligence and reasoning ability. However, it is by understanding his emotions that parents can be of the greatest help. While the child will normally experience strong instinctive urges with which every human being is endowed, he must be prepared to live in a civilized community which often frowns upon the expression of these drives in an uncontrolled fashion.

Overindulgent parents and those who are completely permissive, allowing the child unlimited expression of every impulse, certainly give him distorted ideas of life which he will find increasingly difficult to correct. No child can grow up doing exactly as he pleases without experiencing rather severe emotional traumata. Each child must learn some degree of restraint if he is to live in a group, as he must live. The child must be taught how to cope with fear, anger, jealousy and aggression, for it is only when he is able to manipulate these that he can achieve any degree of growth and independence. When he learns to control his behavior in stressful emotional situations, he is able to achieve a sense of security.

Every child from infancy and throughout life is constantly striving to train his instinctive-emotional drives to coincide with the demands of his environment. All actions which are constantly repeated become habitual, and as such become an inherent part of his behavior. Since habits eventually become an unconscious way of behavior, wholesome habits of thought and action tend to simplify effective living.

All children are impressionable and flexible. The examples set by parents are of great importance in the formation of habits and ways of thinking and acting. Dr. Douglas Thom, one of the leaders in child psychology, said: "The great majority of children with undesirable habits, personality deviations, and delinquent trends are not the products of an irreparable past over which there is no control. They are largely the results of the environment in which they have been reared; and the dominating feature of the environment is always the parent."

All parents exert a powerful influence on their children in helping them to develop a conscience, or superego. In so doing they are laying the foundations of the child's later standards of conduct. All parents, whether they realize it or not, are their children's models for honesty, fair dealings and the acceptance of certain basic values in life. It takes courage to be honest, and the child should be helped to face reality when he must make an ethical decision. He should be taught that he must abide by the consequences after the decision is made.

Mutual trust is necessary for all satisfying personal relationships and the child should be taught to believe in himself. Once he is able to believe in himself he will be able to believe in others. The child who looks for the best qualities in his playmates will always be well liked and popular.

The ability of the child to get along with others is dependent, to a large extent, upon the training the child receives in his early years. Consideration for others must be felt inwardly before it can be expressed convincingly. When parents appreciate a child's thoughtfulness he is encouraged to be thoughtful on other occasions. When this is done often enough, thinking of the comfort of others becomes a habit that is natural. Courtesy toward the child is often more productive of results than merely talking about good manners.

Other qualities that the happily adjusted child possesses are friendliness and tolerance, and these must be felt if they are to be expressed with sincerity. The attitude of the parents should be such as to make it appear reasonable to accept people as they are. When the child has learned this, he has learned a most valuable lesson. Everything should be accepted. When it is pleasant it is to be enjoyed and appreciated. When it is not to the child's liking, it should be accepted tolerantly.

The child can be taught to be courteous to persons who fail to please. Children intuitively sense dislike from others. However, they can learn to counteract this by kindness without insincerity. All children want to be liked, and they can be taught the attitudes by which this can be achieved.

For proper emotional growth the child should have the example of his father as well as that of his mother. From birth the relationship between the father and child should be close and intimate. Fathers should share with mothers the physical and emotional care and guidance of their children. A child's personality needs the influence of both masculine and feminine points of view. This is a very essential part of a child's growth and development.

Obedience is part of the discipline of every child in growing up. While obedience is an important part of child training, it should merely be a background for discipline and not an objective. Obedience, merely for the sake of obedience, is a negative quality. Carried to extremes, habitual obedience stunts the development of independence.

Obedience which is obtained as a result of punishment or

a fear of punishment, is not obedience at all in the true sense of the word. While the parents may regard punishment as a way of teaching, this is not so regarded by the child. To the child punishment is pain inflicted by an older and bigger person, because the child has done something that the adult does not like. Punishment exerts an inhibiting influence on thought and action; it creates resentment and hostility. It does not aid the learning process. Punishment as a rule defeats rather than advances the aims of discipline. It should be used rather infrequently.

Punishment to be effective must be administered when neither the parent nor child is angry. A cooling-off period is most desirable, for during that time the parent may discover the cause of the act, which may or may not merit punishment. It also gives the child time to think about what he did and to realize that what he did was wrong. Usually this will cause him to be willing to make amends or to accept just punishment.

No child should be made to feel the disfavor of his parents for a long time. Neither should he be made to feel undue guilt. Each situation should be handled promptly, and the child should be made to know what he has done wrong, why he deserves the punishment, and what the punishment is supposed to correct.

It should be realized by all parents that no child is born bad. For the child, good and bad, right and wrong, have no actual meaning. The child has to learn what is good and what is bad, what is right and what is wrong. His parents have the task of teaching him how to express his drives, urges and inclinations in such a way as to bring satisfaction to him and at the same time not conflict with the group in which he lives.

Children understand action better than they do words and discussion. Abstract thinking is not developed to any extent in the child. Children seem to know by instinct that persons may say one thing and feel another. A child believes that a grown-up acts the way he feels.

By adhering to the principles that lead to self-realization, by fostering a healthy physical and psychological environment, by love and sympathetic guidance, and by proper example, parents are able to give their children the means of living an effective life. When these are accomplished the child is able to create sufficient inner strength, and thus achieve emotional maturity to face all sorts of situations without experiencing anger, resentment, envy or jealousy.

Bibliography

ALEXANDER, A. J. Commonsense in handling Behavior Problems of Childhood. *Kentucky Medical Journal.* September, 1940, p. 412.

BAKWIN, H. Behavior Problems in Children. *American Journal of Diseases of Children.* Feb., 1946, p. 113.

BENDER, LAURETTA. Aggression in Childhood. *American Journal of Orthopsychiatry.* Dec., 1943, p. 392.

BENDER, LAURETTA, and SCHILDER, PAUL. Aggressiveness in Childhood. *Genetic Psychology Monograph.* XVIII, 1936.

BETTELHEIM, BRUNO. Love Is Not Enough. The Free Press. Glencoe, Illinois, 1951.

BETTELHEIM, BRUNO, and SYLVESTER, EMMY. Notes on the Impact of Parental Occupations: some cultural determinants of symptom choice in emotionally disturbed children. *American Journal of Orthopsychiatry.* Oct., 1950, p. 785.

BEVERLY, B. I. General Principles of Behavior Problems in Children. *Illinois Medical Journal.* Aug., 1941, p. 120.

BRUCH, HILDE. Physiologic and Psychologic Interrelationships in Diabetes in Children. *Psychosomatic Medicine.* Aug., 1949, p. 200.

BRUCH, HILDE, and HEWLETT, IRMA. Psychologic Aspect of the Medical Management of Diabetes in Children. *Psychosomatic Medicine.* May, 1947, p. 205.

BURNS, C. Functional Nervous Disorders in Children. Medical Press. Feb., 1949, p. 597.

CONRAD, S. J. Study of Preschool Children. *Amer. J. Orthopsychiatry.* Mar., 1949, p. 340.

CREAK, M. Hysteria in Childhood. *Brit. J. Child Dis.* Oct., 1939, p. 85.

DUBO, SARA. Psychiatric Study of Children with Pulmonary Tuberculosis. *Amer. J. Orthopsychiatry.* July, 1950, p. 520.

DuBois, F. S. Helping the Child to Grow Up. *Connecticut State Med. J.* Feb., 1950, p. 111.

Dunbar, Flanders. Your Child's Mind and Body. Random House. New York, 1949.

Ferenczi, Sandor. The Unwelcome Child and His Death Instinct. *Internat. J. Psychoanalysis.* Oct., 1929, p. 125.

Fischer, A. E., and Dolger, H. Behavior and Psychologic Problems of Young Diabetic Patients. *Arch. Internal Med.* Dec., 1946, p. 711.

Fodor, Nandor. Emotional Trauma Resulting from Illegitimate Birth. *Arch. Neurol. and Psychiat.* Nov., 1945, p. 381.

Fortes, M. Step-Parenthood and Juvenile Delinquency. *Sociological Review.* March, 1933, p. 153.

Freud, Anna. The Psychoanalytic Study of Infantile Feeding Disturbances. The Psychoanalytic Study of the Child. International Universities Press. New York, 1946, p. 119.

Fries, Margaret E. The Child's Ego Development and the Training of Adults in His Environment. Psychoanalytic Study of the Child. International Universities Press. New York, 1946, p. 85.

Gesell, Arnold. The Embryology of Behavior. Harper, New York.

Gesell, Arnold. The First Five Years of Life. Harper, New York.

Gesell, Arnold. Infancy and Human Growth. Harper, New York.

Gesell, Arnold. The Normal Child and Primary Education. Harper, New York.

Gesell, Arnold. The Retarded Child. Harper, New York.

Gesell, Arnold. Wolf Child and Human Child. Harper, New York.

Gesell, Arnold, and Ilg, Frances L. The Child from Five to Ten. Harper, New York, 1946.

Gesell, Arnold and Ilg, Frances L. Infant and Child in the Culture of Today. Harper, New York.

Harms, E. Handbook of Child Guidance. Child Care Publications. New York, 1947.

Heilpern, Elsie P. Psychologic Problems of Stepchildren. *Psychoanalytic Rev.* April, 1943, p. 163.

HEINILD, S. Incidence of Psychosomatic Illness in Children. *Acta. Paed.* Sept., 1949, p. 117.

HENRY, JULES, and WARSON, SAMUEL. Family Structure and Psychic Development. *The Amer. J. Orthopsychiatry.* Jan., 1951, p. 59.

HOHMAN, L. B. As the Twig Is Bent. The Macmillan Co., New York, 1940.

JOSSELYN, I. M. Emotional Implications of Rheumatic Heart Disease in Children. *Amer. J. Orthopsychiatry.* Jan., 1949, p. 87.

KANNER, LEO. Child Psychiatry. Charles C. Thomas. Springfield, Illinois, 1948.

KAPLAN, M. Approach to Psychiatric Problems in Childhood. *Amer. J. Dis. Ch.* April, 1950, p. 791.

KLEIN, MELANIE. The Psychoanalysis of Children. Hogarth Press. London, 1937.

KNIGHT, R. P. Behavior Problems and Habit Disturbances in Preadolescent Children. *Bull. Menninger Clinic.* Nov., 1944, p. 188.

KORNITZER, MARGARET. Child Adoption in the Modern World. Putnam. London, 1952.

LAMB, W. F. Some Behavior Problems in Infancy and Early Childhood. *Kentucky Medical Journal.* Dec., 1940, p. 584.

LEVY, D. M. Psychic Trauma of Operations. *Am. J. Dis. Ch.* Feb., 1945, p. 7.

LOEWY, HERTA. The Retarded Child. Philosophical Library. New York, 1951.

LURIE, L. A. Child Guidance Procedures. Child Care Publications. New York, 1947.

LURIE, L. A. Somatopsychic Aspects of Behavior Disorders in Children. *Medical Clinics of North America.* 1947, p. 668.

LURIE, L. A. and LURIE, M. Psychoses in Children. *J. Ped.* Aug., 1950, p. 801.

MASSLER, M. and MALONE, A. J. Nailbiting. *J. Ped.* Feb., 1950, p. 523.

MERIAM, ADELE S. Stepfather in the Family. *Social Service Review.* Dec., 1940, p. 655.

MORGAN, G. D. Physiological Instability in Children. *J. Ment. Sc.* Nov., 1949, p. 949.

ODLUM, D. Modern Treatment of Hysteria in Childhood. Med. Press. June, 1948, p. 121.

PACELLA, B. L. Behavior Problems in Children. *Medical Clinics of North America.* May, 1948, p. 655.

PEARSON, G. H. J. Emotional Disorders of Children. W. W. Norton. New York, 1949.

PODOLSKY, EDWARD. Diabetes in Children. *Health.* Dec., 1947, p. 10.

PODOLSKY, EDWARD. The Maladjusted Child. *Archives of Pediatrics.* Jan., 1951, p. 11.

PODOLSKY, EDWARD. The Mentally Ill Child. *Journal of School Health.* September, 1950, p. 197.

PODOLSKY, EDWARD. Training the Child to Acquire Regular Habits. *American Baby.* Jan., 1948, p. 4.

PODOLSKY, EDWARD. What Growing Up Means to a Child. *Baby Post.* Fall 1948, p. 16.

RANK, B., and KAPLAN, S. Case of Pseudoschizophrenia in a Child. *Amer. J. Orthopsychiatry.* July, 1951, p. 155.

REDL, FRITZ, and WINEMAN, DAVID. Children Who Hate. The Free Press. Glencoe, Illinois, 1951.

RIBBLE, MARGARET. The Rights of Infants. Columbia University Press, New York, 1944.

ROSE, J. A. Personality Development of the Child. *Quarterly Journal of Child Behavior.* Jan., 1950, p. 49.

RUBINSTEIN, E. Childhood Mental Diseases in America. *Amer. J. Orthopsychiatry.* March, 1948, p. 314.

SMITH, WILLIAM C. Adjustment Problems of the Stepchild. *Proceedings of the Pacific Northwest Annual Conference on Family Relations.* 1948, p. 87.

SONTAG, L. W. Psychosomatic Patterns in Childhood. *Amer. J. Orthopsychiatry.* Sept., 1950, p. 479.

SPERLING, M. Role of the Mother in Psychosomatic Disorders in Children. *Psychosomatic Med.* Sept., 1949, p. 377.

SPITZ, R. Psychiatric Therapy in Infancy. *Amer. J. Orthopsychiatry.* Nov., 1950, p. 623.

SPOCK, B. Avoiding Behavior Problems. *J. of Ped.* Oct., 1945, p. 363.

SPOCK, B. Baby and Child Care. Duell, Sloan and Pearce. New York, 1945.

SPOCK, B. Common Behavior Disturbances in the First Two Years of life. *J.A.M.A.* March 20, 1948, p. 811.

THOM, DOUGLAS. Everyday Problems of the Everyday Child. D. Appleton and Company, New York, 1927.

WALKER, C. Hysteria in Childhood. *Amer. J. Orthopsychiatry.* Sept., 1947, p. 468.

WEISNER, W. Preventive Psychiatry in Pediatrics. *Arch. of Pediatrics.* March, 1950, p. 311.

WERTHAM, FREDERICK. Psychological Effects of School Segregation. *American Journal of Psychotherapy.* Jan., 1952, p. 94.

WINN, A. Encyclopedia of Child Guidance. Philosophical Library. New York, 1944.

WITMER, HELEN. Psychiatric Interviews with Children. *Commonwealth Fund.* New York, 1946.

WITTMAN, ROBERT. A Pampered Child and His Stepmother. *International Journal of Individual Psychology.* Fourth Quarter. 1936, p. 180.

WOODS SCHOOLS: List of Publications, Langhorne, Pa.